5
INGREDIENT
RECIPES

TASTE OF HOME BOOKS • RDA ENTHUSIAST BRANDS, LLC • MILWAUKEE, WI

**PLUM-GLAZED
COUNTRY RIBS
PG 52**

International Standard Book Number:
978-1-61765-799-3

Library of Congress Control Number:
2018947082

Component Number:
116000239H

Cover Photographer: Grace Natoli Sheldon
Set Stylist: Stacey Genaw
Food Stylist: Shanon Roum

Pictured on front cover:
Bacon & Spinach Pizza, page 42

Pictured on title page:
Smothered Burritos, page 55

Pictured on back cover (from top):
Mediterranean Chicken, page 68
Chili-Lime Roasted Chickpeas, page 8
Shoofly Cupcakes, page 99

Printed in China.
1 3 5 7 9 10 8 6 4 2

TABLE OF CONTENTS

43

85

GET SOCIAL WITH US!

Like Us
facebook.com/tasteofhome

Follow Us
@tasteofhome

Pin Us
pinterest.com/taste_of_home

Tweet Us
twitter.com/tasteofhome

To find a recipe
tasteofhome.com

To submit a recipe
tasteofhome.com/submit

To find out about other *Taste of Home* **products**
shoptasteofhome.com

GREAT MEALS WITH ONLY 5 INGREDIENTS

You don't need an exhaustive list of items to create a delicious homemade dinner. Instead, put a little money back in your wallet and a lot of time back in your schedule with the delectable dishes in ***Taste of Home 5 Ingredient Recipes!***

This handy collection offers 149 family favorites that are easy to make and promise to please. They all come together with no more than five ingredients (with the exceptions you'll find listed in "Take 5!" on the next page). That means you're all set to spend less time at the supermarket and in the kitchen—and less money on grocery bills. What could be better?

Satisfying mains, quick side dishes, no-fuss soups and last-minute desserts...they're all here, and they're all sure to create the sorts of menus friends and family crave. With the brand-new ***5 Ingredient Recipes*** at your fingertips, you're just moments away from full-flavored comfort foods with only a fraction of the work.

Family Classic

Looking for an impressive bite that's sure to satisfy everyone at the table? Keep an eye out for the "Family Classic" icon. These are the all-time favorites, recipes that families have enjoyed for generations, pared down to take advantage of short ingredient lists.

1. Think fresh. Many classic dishes have short ingredient lists. Start with good-quality ingredients, and you won't need to add a lot of extras.

2. Consider ingredients that pile on the flavor. Jarred sauces, packaged rice mixes, seasoning blends, tomatoes with herbs and canned soups give you a head start.

3. Use mixes in new ways. You can make cookies and bars from cake mix, but that's just the beginning. Biscuit and cookie mixes can provide inspiration for a new recipe, too. Let your imagination roam.

4. Check out prepared foods at the store. Just because food is already cooked doesn't mean you need to serve it as is. Cakes from the bakery section, rotisserie chicken from the deli—use these as a starting point.

5. Make convenience products— stuffing, rice, pasta mixes—your own with just a handful of fresh ingredients. Try adding chopped fresh apple, celery and onion to a stuffing mix, or grilled chicken or shrimp to a rice mix.

TAKE 5!

There are a few items that *Taste of Home* doesn't include in five-ingredient counts. They're the essential ingredients that every kitchen should always have on hand, so you don't need to add them to your shopping list.

- **WATER**

- **SALT**
  Both traditional table salt and kosher salt are fine for cooking. Coarser kosher salt gives a more predictable and consistent "pinch" measure; fine-grained table salt is better for passing around at the table.

- **PEPPER**
  Black pepper is the go-to kitchen staple. For the freshest flavor, get a pepper grinder and crack the pepper each time as you cook or serve food.

- **OIL**
  It's a great idea to always have both extra virgin olive oil and vegetable oil (such as canola) in your pantry.

Optional items also are not included when counting ingredients. You'll find wonderful ideas for garnishes, but they aren't necessary to make and enjoy the recipe. Besides, you can always swap them out for your own wonderfully creative touches!

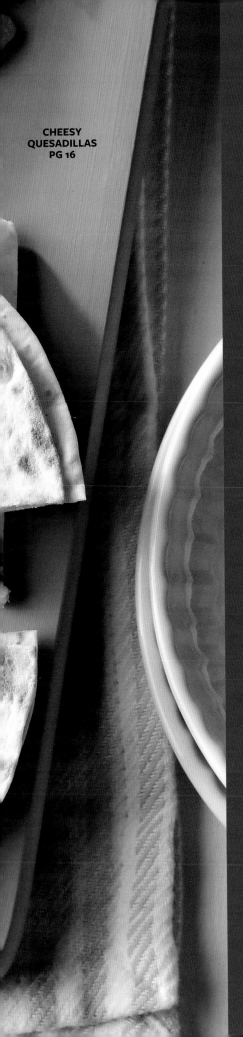

CHEESY
QUESADILLAS
PG 16

Appetizers & Snacks

Party time doesn't necessarily mean
spending extra time in the kitchen. Live it up
with these swift and savory crowd-pleasers.

CHILI-LIME
ROASTED
CHICKPEAS

CHILI-LIME ROASTED CHICKPEAS

Looking for a lighter snack that's still a party pleaser? You've found it! These zesty, crunchy chickpeas will be sure to have everyone happily munching.
—Julie Ruble, Charlotte, NC

Prep: 10 min. • **Bake:** 40 min. + cooling
Makes: 2 cups

- 2 **cans (15 oz. each) chickpeas, rinsed, drained and patted dry**
- 2 **Tbsp. extra virgin olive oil**
- 1 **Tbsp. chili powder**
- 2 **tsp. ground cumin**
- 1 **tsp. grated lime zest**
- 1 **Tbsp. lime juice**
- ¾ **tsp. sea salt**

1. Preheat the oven to 400°. Line a 15x10x1-in. baking sheet with foil. Spread chickpeas in a single layer over foil, removong any loose skins. Bake until very crunchy, 40-45 minutes, stirring every 15 minutes.
2. Meanwhile, whisk the remaining ingredients. Remove chickpeas from the oven; let cool 5 minutes. Drizzle with the oil mixture; shake pan to coat. Cool completely. Store in an airtight container.
⅓ cup: 178 cal., 8g fat (1g sat. fat), 0mg chol., 463mg sod., 23g carb. (3g sugars, 6g fiber), 6g pro.

Orange-Curry Chickpeas Prepare chickpeas according to step 1. Whisk 2 Tbsp. extra virgin olive oil, 1 tsp. grated orange zest and 1 Tbsp. curry powder. Toss beans with oil mixture. Cool.
Lemon-Pepper Chickpeas Prepare chickpeas according to step 1. Whisk 2 Tbsp. extra virgin olive oil, 1 tsp. grated lemon zest and 2 tsp. freshly cracked pepper. Toss beans with oil mixture. Cool.
Rosemary-Sea Salt Chickpeas Prepare chickpeas according to step 1. Toss beans with 2 Tbsp. extra virgin olive oil, 1 Tbsp. minced fresh rosemary and ½ tsp. sea salt. Cool.

GARLIC-HERB MINI QUICHES

Looking for wonderful little bites to dress up the appetizer buffet? Give these cute, delectable tartlets a shot!
—Josephine Piro, Easton, PA

Takes: 25 min. • **Makes:** 45 mini quiches

- 1 pkg. (6½ oz.) reduced-fat garlic-herb spreadable cheese
- ¼ cup fat-free milk
- 2 large eggs
- 3 pkg. (1.9 oz. each) frozen miniature phyllo tart shells
- 2 Tbsp. minced fresh parsley
   Minced chives, optional

1. Preheat oven to 350°. In a small bowl, beat the spreadable cheese, milk and eggs. Place tart shells on an ungreased baking sheet; fill each with 2 tsp. mixture. Sprinkle with parsley.
2. Bake for 10-12 minutes or until the filling is set and shells are lightly browned. Sprinkle with chives if desired. Serve mini quiches warm.
1 mini quiche: 31 cal., 2g fat (0 sat. fat), 12mg chol., 32mg sod., 2g carb. (0 sugars, 0 fiber), 1g pro.
Crab Rangoon Tartlets Substitute 8 oz. whipped cream cheese and 2 Tbsp. sour cream for the spreadable cheese and milk. Omit eggs. Stir in ½ cup flaked crab. Bake as directed.
Smoky Apricot Tartlets Heat 2¼ cups apricot preserves, 1½ tsp. pumpkin pie spice and 3 Tbsp. brown sugar until sugar is dissolved. Spoon into the tart shells. Sprinkle with 1½ cups shredded smoked mozzarella cheese and 3 Tbsp. brown sugar. Bake 5-7 minutes or until the cheese is melted.

LIKE 'EM HOT WINGS

LIKE 'EM HOT WINGS

Who doesn't love wings? And these spicy ones are wonderfully seasoned. You just might have to double the recipe.
—Myra Innes, Auburn, KS

Prep: 10 min. • **Bake:** 30 min.
Makes: about 2 dozen

- 2½ lbs. chicken wings
- 1 bottle (2 oz.) hot pepper sauce (about ¼ cup)
- 1 to 2 garlic cloves, minced
- 1½ tsp. dried rosemary, crushed
- 1 tsp. dried thyme
- ¼ tsp. salt
- ¼ tsp. pepper
   Celery sticks, carrot sticks and blue cheese salad dressing, optional

1. Preheat oven to 425°. Cut chicken wings into three sections; discard wing tips. In a large resealable plastic bag, combine the hot pepper sauce, garlic and seasonings. Add wings; toss to evenly coat. Transfer to a well-greased 13x9-in. baking dish.
2. Bake, uncovered, 30-40 minutes or until chicken juices run clear, turning every 10 minutes. Serve with veggies and dressing if desired.
Note: Uncooked chicken wing sections (wingettes) may be substituted for whole chicken wings.
1 serving: 43 cal., 3g fat (1g sat. fat), 12mg chol., 51mg sod., 0 carb. (0 sugars, 0 fiber), 4g pro.

CHICKEN CHILI WONTON BITES

CHICKEN CHILI WONTON BITES

Everyone needs a surefire, grab-and-go appetizer. These wonton wrappers filled with chicken and spices are mine. They're great for any and all tailgates.
—Heidi Jobe, Carrollton, GA

Takes: 30 min. • **Makes:** 3 dozen

- 36 wonton wrappers
- ½ cup buttermilk ranch salad dressing
- 1 envelope reduced-sodium chili seasoning mix
- 1½ cups shredded rotisserie chicken
- 1 cup shredded sharp cheddar cheese
  Sour cream and sliced green onions, optional

1. Preheat oven to 350°. Press wonton wrappers into greased miniature muffin cups. Bake cups for 4-6 minutes or until lightly browned.

2. In a small bowl, mix salad dressing and seasoning mix; add the chicken and toss to coat. Spoon 1 Tbsp. filling into each wonton cup. Sprinkle with cheese.

3. Bake for 8-10 minutes longer or until heated through and wrappers are golden brown. Serve warm. If desired, top the wonton bites with sour cream and green onions before serving.

1 appetizer: 67 cal., 3g fat (1g sat. fat), 10mg chol., 126mg sod., 6g carb. (0 sugars, 0 fiber), 3g pro.

Mini Reuben Cups Prepare and bake wonton cups as directed. Mix ½ pound chopped deli corned beef, ½ cup sauerkraut (rinsed and well drained) and ½ cup Thousand Island salad dressing; spoon into wonton cups. Sprinkle with 1 cup shredded Swiss cheese. Bake cups as directed.

Egg Salad Wonton Cups Prepare wonton cups as directed; bake for 10-12 minutes or until golden brown. Cook and crumble 10 bacon strips; mix with 3 cups egg salad and ⅓ cup each chopped green onions and shredded carrot. Spoon into wonton cups. Garnish with sliced cherry tomatoes if desired.

✱
TEST KITCHEN TIP
When working with wonton wrappers, try to move quickly. Fill wontons one at a time, keeping the others covered with a damp paper towel until ready to use; otherwise, they could dry out.

SAUSAGE PINWHEELS

These spirals are simple to make but look extra-special on a buffet. Our guests just love them, so I serve the pinwheels often. No one suspects the savory appetizers call for only three ingredients.
—Gail Sykora, Menomonee Falls, WI

Takes: 30 min. • **Makes:** 1 dozen

- 1 tube (8 oz.) refrigerated crescent rolls
- ½ lb. uncooked bulk pork sausage
- 2 Tbsp. minced chives

1. Preheat oven to 375°. Unroll crescent dough onto a lightly floured surface; press perforations to seal. Roll into a 14x10-in. rectangle.
2. Spread sausage to within ½ in. of the edges. Sprinkle with the chives. Roll up carefully jelly-roll style, starting with a long side; pinch seam to seal. Cut into 12 slices; place 1 in. apart in ungreased 15x10x1-in. pan.
3. Bake until golden brown and sausage is cooked through, 12-16 minutes.
1 pinwheel: 132 cal., 9g fat (3g sat. fat), 13mg chol., 293mg sod., 8g carb. (1g sugars, 0 fiber), 4g pro.

WALNUT & FIG GOAT CHEESE LOG

Here's a simple spread you can put together in minutes.
—Ana-Marie Correll, Hollister, CA

Prep: 10 min. + chilling • **Makes:** 1⅓ cups

- 2 logs (4 oz. each) fresh goat cheese
- 8 dried figs, finely chopped
- ½ cup finely chopped walnuts, toasted, divided
- ¾ tsp. pepper
- 1 Tbsp. honey, optional
  Assorted crackers

In a small bowl, crumble cheese. Stir in the figs, ¼ cup walnuts, pepper and, if desired, honey. Shape mixture into a log, about 6 in. long. Roll log in remaining walnuts. Refrigerate 4 hours or overnight. Serve with crackers.
2 Tbsp: 93 cal., 7g fat (2g sat. fat), 15mg chol., 92mg sod., 6g carb. (3g sugars, 1 fiber), 3g pro.

SAUSAGE PINWHEELS

SAVORY POTATO SKINS

SAVORY POTATO SKINS

Potato skins have been a family and restaurant sure-thing for a long time—with good reason. So put together a plate of these classics and make movie night, game day or holiday buffets extra special.
—Andrea Holcomb, Torrington, CT

Prep: 1¼ hours • **Broil:** 5 min.
Makes: 32 appetizers

- 4   large baking potatoes (about 12 oz. each)
- 3   Tbsp. butter, melted
- 1   tsp. salt
- 1   tsp. garlic powder
- 1   tsp. paprika
     Sour cream and chives, optional

1. Preheat oven to 375°. Scrub potatoes; pierce several times with a fork. Place on a greased baking sheet; bake until tender, 1 to 1¼ hours. Cool slightly.
2. Cut each potato lengthwise in half. Scoop out pulp, leaving ¼-in. thick shells (save pulp for another use).
3. Cut each half shell lengthwise into quarters; return to baking sheet. Brush insides with butter. Mix the seasonings; sprinkle over butter.
4. Broil 4-5 in. from heat until golden brown, 5-8 minutes. If desired, mix sour cream and chives and serve with the potato skins.
1 appetizer: 56 cal., 2g fat (1g sat. fat), 6mg chol., 168mg sod., 8g carb. (0 sugars, 1g fiber), 1g pro.

FONTINA ASPARAGUS TART

FONTINA ASPARAGUS TART

This lemony tart is loaded with fontina cheese and fresh asparagus. It's a snap to make but looks really impressive. Be warned—your guests will be vying for the last tasty slice.
—Heidi Meek, Grand Rapids, MI

Prep: 15 min. • **Bake:** 20 min.
Makes: 16 servings

- 1   lb. fresh asparagus, trimmed
- 1   sheet frozen puff pastry, thawed
- 2   cups shredded fontina cheese
- 1   tsp. grated lemon peel
- 2   Tbsp. lemon juice
- 1   Tbsp. olive oil
- ¼   tsp. salt
- ¼   tsp. pepper

1. Preheat oven to 400°. In a large skillet, bring 1 in. of water to a boil; add the asparagus. Cook, covered, until crisp-tender, 3-5 minutes. Drain and pat dry.
2. On a lightly floured surface, roll pastry sheet into a 16x12-in. rectangle. Transfer to a parchment paper-lined large baking sheet. Bake until golden brown, about 10 minutes.
3. Sprinkle 1½ cups cheese over pastry to within ½-in. of edges. Place asparagus over top; sprinkle with remaining cheese. Mix remaining ingredients; drizzle over top. Bake until cheese is melted, about 10-15 minutes. Serve warm.
1 serving: 142 cal., 9g fat (4g sat. fat), 16mg chol., 202mg sod., 10g carb. (1g sugars, 1g fiber), 5g pro.

RISOTTO BALLS

ROASTED VEGETABLE DIP

While my children were always very willing eaters, I came up with this recipe to get them to eat more veggies. The dip doesn't last long in our house!
—Sarah Vasques, Milford, NH

Prep: 15 min. • **Bake:** 25 min. + cooling
Makes: 20 servings (2 Tbsp. each)

- 2 large sweet red peppers
- 1 large zucchini
- 1 medium onion
- 1 Tbsp. olive oil
- ½ tsp. salt
- ¼ tsp. pepper
- 1 pkg. (8 oz.) reduced-fat cream cheese
  Assorted crackers or fresh vegetables

1. Preheat oven to 425°. Cut vegetables into 1-in. pieces. Place in a 15x10x1-in. baking pan coated with cooking spray; toss with oil, salt and pepper. Roast about 25-30 minutes or until tender, stirring occasionally. Cool completely.
2. Place vegetables and cream cheese in a food processor; process until blended. Transfer to a bowl; refrigerate, covered, until serving. Serve with crackers.
2 Tbsp. dip: 44 cal., 3g fat (2g sat. fat), 8mg chol., 110mg sod., 3g carb. (2g sugars, 1g fiber), 2g pro.

DID YOU KNOW?
Roasted veggies account for more than half the volume of this blended dip, which means fewer calories, less saturated fat, more nutrients—and an amazing flavor. Try it as a spread for bagels, too.

RISOTTO BALLS

Also known as Arancini, these rice balls freeze well, so I make them long before the party. My Italian grandma made them for me. I still ask for them when I visit her.
—Gretchen Whelan, San Francisco, CA

Prep: 35 min. • **Bake:** 25 min.
Makes: about 3 dozen

- 1½ cups water
- 1 cup uncooked arborio rice
- 1 tsp. salt
- 2 large eggs, lightly beaten
- ⅔ cup sun-dried tomato pesto
- 2 cups panko (Japanese) bread crumbs, divided
  Marinara sauce, warmed

1. Preheat the oven to 375°. In a large saucepan, combine water, rice and salt; bring to a boil. Reduce heat; simmer, covered, 18-20 minutes or until liquid is absorbed and rice is tender. Let stand, covered, 10 minutes. Transfer to a large bowl; cool slightly. Add eggs and pesto; stir in 1 cup bread crumbs.
2. Place the remaining bread crumbs in a shallow bowl. Shape rice mixture into 1¼-in. balls. Roll in bread crumbs, patting to help coating adhere. Place on greased 15x10x1-in. baking pans. Bake 25-30 minutes or until golden brown. Serve with marinara sauce.
1 appetizer: 42 cal., 1g fat (0 sat. fat), 10mg chol., 125mg sod., 7g carb. (1g sugars, 0 fiber), 1g pro. **Diabetic exchanges:** ½ starch.

SLOPPY JOE NACHOS

When my kids were little, they adored snacks they could eat with their fingers. Use this for a treat—or a fast meal.
—Janet Rhoden, Hortonville, WI

Takes: 15 min. • **Makes:** 6 servings

- 1   lb. ground beef
- 1   can (15½ oz.) sloppy joe sauce
- 1   pkg. (12 oz.) tortilla chips
- ¾   cup shredded cheddar cheese
- ¼   cup sliced ripe olives, optional

1. In a large skillet, cook the beef over medium heat until no longer pink; drain. Add sloppy joe sauce; cook, uncovered, for 5 minutes or until heated through.

2. Arrange tortilla chips on a serving plate. Top with meat mixture, cheese and, if desired, olives.

1 serving: 482 cal., 23g fat (8g sat. fat), 52mg chol., 790mg sod., 45g carb. (5g sugars, 3g fiber), 21g pro.

MINI FETA PIZZAS

With the basil we grow in our garden, we have an abundance of pesto, but feel free to use purchased pesto if you like. We'll often add extra cheese or garden goodies.
—Nicole Filizetti, Stevens Point, WI

Takes: 20 min. • **Makes:** 4 servings

- 2   whole wheat English muffins, split and toasted
- 2   Tbsp. reduced-fat cream cheese
- 4   tsp. prepared pesto
- ½   cup thinly sliced red onion
- ¼   cup crumbled feta cheese

1. Preheat oven to 425°. Place muffins on a baking sheet.

2. Mix cream cheese and pesto; spread over muffins. Top with onion and feta cheese. Bake until lightly browned, about 6-8 minutes.

1 pizza: 136 cal., 6g fat (3g sat. fat), 11mg chol., 294mg sod., 16g carb. (4g sugars, 3g fiber), 6g pro. **Diabetic exchanges:** 1 starch, 1 fat.

MINI FETA PIZZAS

CHEESY QUESADILLAS

TERIYAKI SALMON BUNDLES

If you're bored with the same old appetizers, give this recipe a try. I serve the little salmon bundles on skewers for easy dipping. Standing the skewers in a small vase filled with table salt makes for a charming and festive presentation.

—Diane Halferty, Corpus Christi, TX

Prep: 30 min. • **Bake:** 20 min.
Makes: 32 appetizers (¾ cup sauce)

    4 Tbsp. reduced-sodium teriyaki
       sauce, divided
    ½ tsp. grated lemon zest
    2 Tbsp. lemon juice
 1¼ lbs. salmon fillet, cut into 1-in. cubes
    1 pkg. (17.3 oz.) frozen puff pastry,
       thawed
   ⅔ cup orange marmalade

1. Preheat oven to 400°. In a large bowl, whisk 2 Tbsp. teriyaki sauce, lemon zest and lemon juice. Add the salmon; toss to coat. Marinate at room temperature for 20 minutes.
2. Drain salmon, discarding marinade. Unfold the puff pastry. Cut each sheet lengthwise into ½-in.-wide strips; cut crosswise in half. Overlap two strips of pastry, forming an X. Place a salmon cube in the center. Wrap pastry over salmon; pinch ends to seal. Place on a greased baking sheet, seam side down. Repeat. Bake 18-20 minutes or until bundles are golden brown.
3. In a small bowl, mix marmalade and the remaining teriyaki. Serve sauce with the salmon bundles.
1 bundle with 1 tsp. sauce: 120 cal., 6g fat (1g sat. fat), 9mg chol., 93mg sod., 13g carb. (4g sugars, 1g fiber), 4g pro.

CHEESY QUESADILLAS
You can slice these into thin wedges for party appetizers or serve them alongside bowls of chili instead of bread.
—Terri Keeney, Greeley, CO

Takes: 15 min. • **Makes:** 6 servings

    4 flour tortillas (8 in.), warmed
 1½ cups shredded Mexican cheese
       blend
    ½ cup salsa

1. Place the tortillas on a greased baking sheet. Combine the cheese and salsa; spread over half of each tortilla. Gently fold over.
2. Broil 4 in. from the heat for 3 minutes on each side or until golden brown. Cut into six wedges.
1 wedge: 223 cal., 11g fat (5g sat. fat), 25mg chol., 406mg sod., 21g carb. (1g sugars, 1g fiber), 9g pro.

Turkey Quesadillas Sprinkle ½ cup diced cooked turkey over the cheese mixture. Proceed as directed.
Mushroom Quesadillas Saute 8 oz. of chopped fresh mushrooms and 1 chopped seeded jalapeno pepper in 1 Tbsp. olive oil until tender and liquid is nearly evaporated. Add 2 Tbsp. minced fresh cilantro; cook and stir for 1 minute. Remove from the heat. Sprinkle cheese over half of each tortilla. Top cheese with mushroom mixture; proceed as directed. Serve with salsa.
Two-Cheese Quesadillas Reduce the cheese to 1 cup and combine with 1 cup shredded part-skim mozzarella cheese. Sprinkle over tortillas as directed. Top as desired with veggies: 1 cup finely chopped tomatoes, ½ cup finely chopped green pepper, ¼ cup chopped onion. Proceed as directed. Serve with salsa if desired.

TERIYAKI SALMON
BUNDLES

BUFFALO CHICKEN POCKETS

BUFFALO CHICKEN POCKETS

Here's my idea of pub food made easy: biscuits flavored with Buffalo wing sauce and blue cheese. They are my all-time Friday night favorite.
—Maria Regakis, Saugus, MA

Takes: 30 min. • **Makes:** 8 servings

- ¾ lb. ground chicken
- ⅓ cup Buffalo wing sauce
- 1 tube (16.3 oz.) large refrigerated buttermilk biscuits
- ½ cup shredded cheddar cheese
  Blue cheese salad dressing, optional

1. Preheat oven to 375°. In a large skillet, cook chicken over medium heat about 5-7 minutes or until no longer pink, breaking into crumbles; drain. Remove from heat; stir in wing sauce.
2. On a floured surface, roll each biscuit into a 6-in. circle; top each with ¼ cup chicken mixture and 2 Tbsp. cheese. Fold dough over filling; pinch edge to seal.
3. Transfer to an ungreased baking sheet. Bake 12-14 minutes or until golden brown. If desired, serve with the blue cheese dressing.
Freeze option: Freeze cooled pockets in a resealable plastic freezer bag. To use, reheat pockets on an ungreased baking sheet in a preheated 375° oven until heated through.
1 pocket: 258 cal., 12g fat (5g sat. fat), 35mg chol., 987mg sod., 25g carb. (3g sugars, 1g fiber), 12g pro.

BEER DIP

BEER DIP

Ranch dressing mix flavors this fast-to-fix specialty that's packed with shredded cheese. Ideal with pretzels, it's one of those snacks that when you start eating it, you can't stop! You can make this dip with any type of beer, including the no-alcohol kind. Someone always asks for the recipe when I take it to parties.
—Michelle Long, New Castle, CO

Takes: 5 min. • **Makes:** 3½ cups

- 2 pkg. (8 oz. each) cream cheese, softened
- ⅓ cup beer or nonalcoholic beer
- 1 envelope ranch salad dressing mix
- 2 cups shredded cheddar cheese
 Pretzels

In a large bowl, beat the cream cheese, beer and dressing mix until smooth. Stir in cheddar cheese. Serve with pretzels.
2 Tbsp. dip: 89 cal., 8g fat (5g sat. fat), 26mg chol., 177mg sod., 1g carb. (0 sugars, 0 fiber), 3g pro.

RASPBERRY-WALNUT BRIE

You need only a few ingredients to make this elegant appetizer; all I usually have to buy is the Brie. It's perfect for a family movie night or an evening with friends.
—Janet Edwards, Beaverton, OR

Takes: 10 min. • **Makes:** 16 servings

- ¼ cup seedless raspberry jam
- 2 rounds (8 oz. each) Brie cheese
- 1 pkg. (11½ oz.) stone ground wheat crackers, divided
- ½ cup finely chopped walnuts
- 1 Tbsp. butter, melted

1. In a small microwave-safe bowl, microwave jam on high for 15-20 seconds or until melted; brush over the Brie.
2. Crush nine crackers. In a small bowl, combine the cracker crumbs, nuts and butter; press into the jam. Serve with remaining crackers.
2 Tbsp.: 236 cal., 15g fat (6g sat. fat), 30mg chol., 367mg sod., 18g carb. (5g sugars, 1g fiber), 9g pro.

BUFFALO
CHICKEN SLIDERS
PG 31

Soups & Sandwiches

Serve up a duo of comfort-food favorites tonight.
After all, this perfect pairing is only a handful of
items—and often just a few minutes— away.

TOMATO STEAK SANDWICHES

TOMATO STEAK SANDWICHES

Once when we were light on groceries, I came up with these open-faced sammies. They've been a favorite ever since.
—Tessa Edwards, Provo, UT

Takes: 20 min. • **Makes:** 6 servings

- 2 tsp. canola oil
- 1 lb. beef top sirloin steak, cut into thin strips
- ⅛ tsp. salt
   Dash pepper
- 3 plain bagels, split
- ⅓ cup cream cheese, softened
- 6 thick slices tomato
- 6 slices part-skim mozzarella cheese

1. Preheat broiler. In a large skillet, heat oil over medium heat. Add beef; cook and stir 3-5 minutes or until browned; drain. Stir in salt and pepper.

2. Spread cut sides of bagels with cream cheese. Transfer to an ungreased baking sheet; layer beef over bagels. Top with the tomato and mozzarella cheese. Broil 4-6 in. from heat 3-5 minutes or until cheese is melted and lightly browned.

1 open-faced sandwich: 381 cal., 15g fat (7g sat. fat), 63mg chol., 544mg sod., 31g carb. (6g sugars, 1g fiber), 30g pro.

WILD RICE & MUSHROOM SOUP

Rich and hearty, this soup is frequently requested at our family get-togethers. It's ready in a flash, and if you're cooking for a vegetarian, simply swap vegetable stock for the beef broth.
—Danielle Noble, Fort Thomas, KY

Prep: 10 min.
Cook: 35 min.
Makes: 8 servings (2 qt.)

- 1 lb. baby portobello mushrooms, chopped
- 2 Tbsp. olive oil
- 2 pkg. (6 oz. each) long grain and wild rice mix
- 1 carton (32 oz.) reduced-sodium beef broth
- ½ cup water
- 2 cups heavy whipping cream

In a Dutch oven, saute mushrooms in oil until tender. Add the rice, contents of seasoning packets, broth and water. Bring to a boil. Reduce heat; cover and simmer for 25 minutes. Add cream and heat through.

1 cup: 399 cal., 26g fat (14g sat. fat), 84mg chol., 803mg sod., 35g carb. (2g sugars, 1g fiber), 8g pro.

SPINACH & WHITE BEAN SOUP

For me, soup is love, comfort, happiness and memories. With all its veggies and beans, this one truly appeals to my kitchen-sink style of cooking.
—Annette Palermo, Beach Haven, NJ

Takes: 30 min. • **Makes:** 6 servings

- 2 tsp. olive oil
- 3 garlic cloves, minced
- 3 cans (15 oz. each) cannellini beans, rinsed and drained, divided
- ¼ tsp. pepper
- 1 carton (32 oz.) vegetable or reduced-sodium chicken broth
- 4 cups chopped fresh spinach (about 3 oz.)
- ¼ cup thinly sliced fresh basil
  Shredded Parmesan cheese, optional

1. In a large saucepan, heat the oil over medium heat. Add garlic; cook and stir 30-45 seconds or until tender. Stir in two cans of beans, pepper and broth.

2. Puree mixture using an immersion blender. Or puree in a blender and return to pan. Stir in the remaining can of beans; bring to a boil. Reduce heat; simmer, covered, 15 minutes, stirring mixture occasionally.

3. Stir in the spinach and basil; cook, uncovered, 2-4 minutes or until spinach is wilted. If desired, serve with cheese.

Note: Reduced-sodium vegetable broth isn't widely available, but the organic versions of big-brand vegetable broths are typically lower in sodium than their conventional versions.

1¼ cups: 192 cal., 2g fat (0 sat. fat), 0 chol., 886mg sod., 33g carb. (1g sugars, 9g fiber), 9g pro.

SPINACH & WHITE BEAN SOUP

SPICY POTATO SOUP

SPICY POTATO SOUP

My sister-in-law passed along this very child-friendly recipe. Since she prefers her foods much spicier than we do, I cut back on the heat by reducing the amount of pepper sauce. Feel free to increase it or add some herbs if you prefer more kick.
—Audrey Wall, Industry, PA

Prep: 20 min.
Cook: 70 min.
Makes: 8 servings (2 qt.)

- 1 lb. ground beef
- 4 cups cubed peeled potatoes (½-in. cubes)
- 1 small onion, chopped
- 3 cans (8 oz. each) tomato sauce
- 4 cups water
- 2 tsp. salt
- 1½ tsp. pepper
- ½ to 1 tsp. hot pepper sauce

In a Dutch oven, brown ground beef over medium heat until no longer pink; drain. Add the potatoes, onion and tomato sauce. Stir in the water, salt, pepper and hot pepper sauce; bring to a boil. Reduce heat and simmer for 1 hour or until the potatoes are tender and the soup has thickened.

1 cup: 159 cal., 5g fat (2g sat. fat), 28mg chol., 764mg sod., 16g carb. (2g sugars, 2g fiber), 12g pro.

KIELBASA CHILI

This easy creation combines the flavors of chili dogs in a bowl! I make it when I need a hot, hearty meal in a hurry. It's also festive looking and a super dish to serve when everyone's there at my house watching football games.
—Audra Duvall, Las Vegas, NV

Takes: 20 min. • **Makes:** 7 servings

- 1 lb. smoked kielbasa or Polish sausage, halved and sliced
- 2 cans (14½ oz. each) diced tomatoes, undrained
- 1 can (15 oz.) chili with beans
- 1 can (8¾ oz.) whole kernel corn, drained
- 1 can (2¼ oz.) sliced ripe olives, drained

In a Dutch oven coated with cooking spray, saute kielbasa until browned. Stir in the remaining ingredients. Bring to a boil. Reduce heat; simmer soup, uncovered, for 4-5 minutes or until heated through.
Freeze option: Cool chili and transfer to freezer containers. Freeze up to 3 months. To use, thaw in the refrigerator. Place in a saucepan; heat through.
1 cup: 319 cal., 20g fat (7g sat. fat), 49mg chol., 1308mg sod., 20g carb. (6g sugars, 5g fiber), 14g pro.

ORANGE TURKEY CROISSANTS

Here's an amazing sandwich that feels special. Sweet and tangy orange and crunchy pecans make it truly delicious.
—Jennifer Moore, Centerville, IA

Takes: 10 min. • **Makes:** 6 servings

6   Tbsp. spreadable cream cheese
6   Tbsp. orange marmalade
6   croissants, split
½   cup chopped pecans
1   lb. thinly sliced deli turkey

Spread cream cheese and marmalade onto bottom half of croissants. Sprinkle with pecans. Top with turkey; replace the tops.
1 sandwich: 479 cal., 25g fat (11g sat. fat), 80mg chol., 1165mg sod., 43g carb. (19g sugars, 3g fiber), 21g pro.

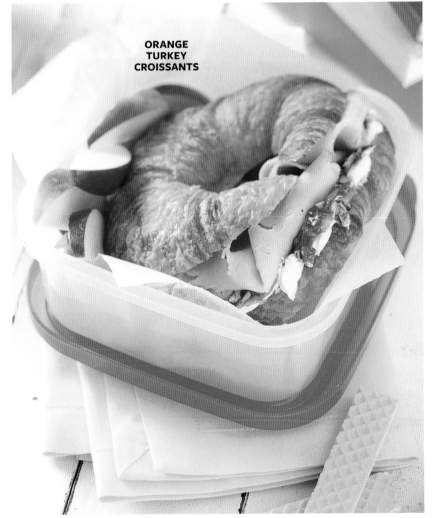

ORANGE TURKEY CROISSANTS

TROPICAL BEEF WRAPS

For my finicky little ones, I create fast, tasty recipes like this tropical wrap. It's a smart, delicious way to use up leftover roast beef.
—Amy Tong, Anaheim, CA

Takes: 15 min. • **Makes:** 4 servings

1   carton (8 oz.) spreadable pineapple cream cheese
4   flour tortillas (10 in.)
4   cups fresh baby spinach (about 4 oz.)
¾   lb. thinly sliced deli roast beef
1   medium mango, peeled and sliced

Spread cream cheese over tortillas to within 1 in. of edges. Layer with spinach, roast beef and sliced mango. Roll up tightly and serve.
1 wrap: 522 cal., 20g fat (10g sat. fat), 100mg chol., 1211mg sod., 58g carb. (21g sugars, 4g fiber), 26g pro.

BEEF MACARONI SOUP

I think you'll love my quick version of classic beef macaroni soup. Loaded with veggies and pasta, it's just as good as if you'd made it all from scratch.
—Debra Baker, Greenville, NC

Takes: 25 min. • **Makes:** 5 servings

1   lb. ground beef
2   cups frozen mixed vegetables
1   can (14½ oz.) diced tomatoes, undrained
1   can (14½ oz.) beef broth
¼   tsp. pepper
½   cup uncooked elbow macaroni

In a large saucepan, cook beef over medium heat until no longer pink; drain. Stir in the mixed vegetables, tomatoes, broth and pepper. Bring to a boil; add macaroni. Reduce the heat; cover and simmer for abouy 8-10 minutes or until macaroni and vegetables are tender.
1 cup: 233 cal., 8g fat (4g sat. fat), 46mg chol., 341mg sod., 19g carb. (6g sugars, 5g fiber), 20g pro. **Diabetic exchanges:** 2 lean meat, 1 starch, 1 vegetable, ½ fat.

CREAMY CHICKEN SOUP

Kids won't resist eating vegetables when this creamy and cheesy quick-fix soup is on the menu.
—LaVonne Lundgren, Sioux City, IA

Takes: 30 min. • **Makes:** 7 servings

4   cups cubed cooked chicken breast
3½ cups water
2   cans (10¾ oz. each) condensed cream of chicken soup, undiluted
1   pkg. (16 oz.) frozen mixed vegetables, thawed
1   can (14½ oz.) diced potatoes, drained
1   pkg. (16 oz.) process cheese (Velveeta), cubed

In a Dutch oven, combine the first five ingredients. Bring to a boil. Reduce heat; cover and simmer for 8-10 minutes or until vegetables are tender. Stir in cheese just until melted (do not boil).
1½ cups: 481 cal., 24g fat (12g sat. fat), 121mg chol., 1650mg sod., 26g carb. (8g sugars, 4g fiber), 39g pro.

PULLED PORK SANDWICHES

Foolproof and wonderfully delicious describes my barbecue pork recipe. Just four ingredients and a slow cooker make a fabulous dish with little effort.
—Sarah Johnson, Chicago, IL

Prep: 15 min.
Cook: 7 hours
Makes: 6 servings

1. lemon-garlic pork loin fillet (about 1⅓ lbs.)
1. can (12 oz.) Dr Pepper
1. bottle (18 oz.) barbecue sauce
6. hamburger buns, split

1. Place pork in a 3-qt. slow cooker. Pour Dr Pepper over top. Cover and cook on low for 7-9 hours or until meat is tender.
2. Remove meat; cool slightly. Discard cooking juices. Shred meat with two forks and return to slow cooker. Stir in barbecue sauce; heat through. Serve on hamburger buns.

Freeze option: Place individual portions of the cooled meat mixture and juice in freezer containers. To use, partially thaw in refrigerator overnight. Microwave, covered, on high in a microwave-safe dish until heated through, gently stirring and adding a little water if necessary.

1 sandwich: 348 cal., 8g fat (2g sat. fat), 45mg chol., 1695mg sod., 43g carb. (22g sugars, 2g fiber), 25g pro.

TEST KITCHEN TIP
To make the most out of a few items, select ingredients that pack a full-flavored punch. This sandwich recipe, for instance, relies on barbecue sauce and a pork loin already seasoned with garlic and lemon.

**PULLED PORK
SANDWICHES**

*Family
Classic*

ROASTED TOMATO SOUP WITH FRESH BASIL

Roasting brings out the tomatoes' rich, sweet flavor in this soup. It has a slightly chunky texture that shows it's fresh and homemade. Summertime basil rounds out the must-try dish.
—Marie Forte, Raritan, NJ

Prep: 20 min. • **Bake:** 25 min.
Makes: 6 servings

- 3½ lbs. tomatoes (about 11 medium), halved
- 1 small onion, quartered
- 2 garlic cloves, peeled and halved
- 2 Tbsp. olive oil
- 2 Tbsp. fresh thyme leaves
- 1 tsp. salt
- ¼ tsp. pepper
- 12 fresh basil leaves
  Salad croutons and thinly sliced fresh basil, optional

1. Preheat oven to 400°. Place tomatoes, onion and garlic in a greased 15x10x1-in. baking pan; drizzle with oil. Sprinkle with the thyme, salt and pepper; toss to coat. Roast for 25-30 minutes or until tender, stirring once. Cool slightly.
2. Process tomato mixture and basil leaves in batches in a blender until smooth. Transfer to a large saucepan; heat soup through. If desired, top with croutons and sliced basil.
1 cup: 107 cal., 5g fat (1g sat. fat), 0 chol., 411mg sod., 15g carb. (9g sugars, 4g fiber), 3g pro. **Diabetic exchanges:** 1 starch, 1 fat.

BACON-POTATO CORN CHOWDER

BACON-POTATO CORN CHOWDER

I was raised on a farm, and a warm soup with homey ingredients like this one was always a treat after a chilly day outside. My hearty chowder nourishes the family.
—Katie Lillo, Big Lake, MN

Takes: 30 min. • **Makes:** 6 servings

- ½ lb. bacon strips, chopped
- ¼ cup chopped onion
- 1½ lbs. Yukon Gold potatoes (about 5 medium), peeled and cubed
- 1 can (14¾ oz.) cream-style corn
- 1 can (12 oz.) evaporated milk
- ¼ tsp. salt
- ¼ tsp. pepper

1. In a large skillet, cook bacon over medium heat until crisp, stirring occasionally. Remove with a slotted spoon; drain on paper towels. Discard drippings, reserving 1½ tsp. in pan. Add onion to drippings; cook and stir over medium-high heat until tender.
2. Meanwhile, place potatoes in a large saucepan; add water to cover. Bring to a boil over high heat. Reduce heat to medium; cook potatoes, uncovered, 10-15 minutes or until tender. Drain, reserving 1 cup potato water.
3. Add the corn, milk, salt, pepper and reserved potato water to saucepan; heat through. Stir in bacon and onion.
1 cup: 271 cal., 11g fat (5g sat. fat), 30mg chol., 555mg sod., 34g carb. (9g sugars, 2g fiber), 10g pro.

COLORFUL CHICKEN & SQUASH SOUP

When I turned 40, I decided I wanted to live a healthier lifestyle, which included cooking light for my family. I make this soup every week, and everyone loves it.
—Trina Bigham, Fairhaven, MA

Prep: 25 min. • **Cook:** 1½ hours
Makes: 14 servings (5¼ qt.)

- 1 broiler/fryer chicken (4 lbs.), cut up
- 13 cups water
- 5 lbs. butternut squash, peeled and cubed (about 10 cups)
- 1 bunch kale, trimmed and chopped
- 6 medium carrots, chopped
- 2 large onions, chopped
- 3 tsp. salt

1. Place chicken and water in a stockpot. Bring to a boil. Reduce heat; cover and simmer for 1 hour or until the chicken is tender.
2. Remove chicken from broth. Strain broth and skim fat. Return broth to the pan; add the squash, kale, carrots and onions. Bring to a boil. Reduce heat; cover and simmer for 25-30 minutes or until vegetables are tender.
3. When the chicken is cool enough to handle, remove meat from bones and cut into bite-size pieces. Discard the chicken bones and skin. Add the meat and salt to soup; heat through.
1½ cups: 228 cal., 8g fat (2g sat. fat), 50mg chol., 579mg sod., 22g carb. (6g sugars, 6g fiber), 18g pro. **Diabetic exchanges:** 2 lean meat, 1 starch, 1 vegetable, ½ fat.

★ ★ ★ ★ ★ **READER REVIEW**
"I love how versatile this soup is. You can use chard or spinach, you can add white beans, and you can switch from butternut squash to pumpkin or even sweet potatoes."
PCJD TASTEOFHOME.COM

GREEK TOMATO SOUP WITH ORZO

My recipe for manestra, *which means "orzo" in Greek, is this straightforward and very easy to make recipe. Just a few steps transform simple ingredients into a creamy, tomatoey one-pot-wonder that's ready in 35 minutes.*
—Kiki Vagianos, Melrose, MA

Prep: 10 min. • **Cook:** 25 min.
Makes: 4 servings

- 2 Tbsp. olive oil
- 1 medium onion, chopped
- 1¼ cups uncooked whole wheat orzo pasta
- 2 cans (14½ oz. each) whole tomatoes, undrained, coarsely chopped
- 3 cups reduced-sodium chicken broth
- 2 tsp. dried oregano
- ¼ tsp. salt
- ¼ tsp. pepper
  Crumbled feta cheese and minced fresh basil, optional

1. In large saucepan, heat the olive oil over medium heat; saute the onion until tender, 3-5 minutes. Add orzo; cook and stir until lightly toasted.
2. Stir in tomatoes, broth and seasonings; bring to a boil. Reduce heat; simmer the soup, covered, until orzo is tender, 15-20 minutes, stirring occasionally. If desired, top with feta and basil.
Freeze option: Freeze cooled soup in freezer containers. To use, partially thaw in refrigerator overnight. Heat through in a saucepan, stirring occasionally and adding a little broth or water if necessary.
1 cup: 299 cal., 8g fat (1g sat. fat), 0 chol., 882mg sod., 47g carb. (7g sugars, 12g fiber), 11g pro.

GREEK TOMATO SOUP WITH ORZO

ITALIAN BEEF
HOAGIES

ITALIAN BEEF HOAGIES

You'll need just five ingredients to feed a crowd these tender tangy sandwiches. On weekends, I start the roast the night before, so I can shred it in the morning.
—Lori Piatt, Danville, IL

Prep: 25 min. • **Cook:** 8 hours
Makes: 18 servings

- 1 beef sirloin tip roast (4 lbs.), halved
- 2 envelopes Italian salad dressing mix
- 2 cups water
- 1 jar (16 oz.) mild pickled pepper rings, undrained
- 18 hoagie buns, split

1. Place the roast in a 5-qt. slow cooker. Combine the salad dressing mix and water; pour over roast. Cover and cook on low for 8-10 hours or until the meat is tender.
2. Remove meat; shred with two forks and return to the slow cooker. Add the pepper rings; heat through. Spoon ½ cup meat mixture onto each bun.

1 sandwich: 346 cal., 9g fat (4g sat. fat), 53mg chol., 674mg sod., 39g carb. (8g sugars, 2g fiber), 26g pro.

OVEN-BAKED BURGERS

A crispy coating mix is the top-secret ingredient that dresses up these burgers. You bake in the oven instead of grilling or frying. I like to use a sweet and spicy steak sauce for the best flavor.
—Mike Goldman, Arden Hills, MN

Takes: 30 min.
Makes: 4 servings

- ¼ cup steak sauce
- 2 Tbsp. plus ⅓ cup seasoned coating mix, divided
- 1 lb. ground beef
- 4 hamburger buns, split
- 4 lettuce leaves

1. Preheat oven to 350°. In a large bowl, combine steak sauce and 2 Tbsp. of the coating mix. Crumble beef over mixture; mix well. Shape into four 3½-in. patties.
2. Dip both sides of patties in remaining coating. Place patties on an ungreased baking sheet.
3. Bake until a thermometer reads 160°, about 20 minutes, turning once. Serve on buns with lettuce.

1 burger: 403 cal., 17g fat (6g sat. fat), 70mg chol., 889mg sod., 35g carb. (6g sugars, 1g fiber), 26g pro.

**COCONUT CURRY
CAULIFLOWER SOUP**

COCONUT CURRY CAULIFLOWER SOUP

When I'm in need of comfort food, I stir up a velvety batch of this Asian-spiced soup. Then I finish it with a sprinkle of cilantro over the top.
—Elizabeth DeHart, West Jordan, UT

Prep: 10 min. • **Cook:** 25 min.
Makes: 10 servings (2½ qt.)

- 2 Tbsp. olive oil
- 1 medium onion, finely chopped
- 3 Tbsp. yellow curry paste
- 2 medium heads cauliflower, broken into florets
- 1 carton (32 oz.) vegetable broth
- 1 cup coconut milk
  Minced fresh cilantro, optional

1. In a large saucepan, heat the oil over medium heat. Add onion; cook and stir until softened, 2-3 minutes. Add curry paste; cook until fragrant, 1-2 minutes. Add cauliflower and broth. Increase heat to high; bring to a boil. Reduce the heat to medium-low; cook mixture, covered, about 20 minutes.
2. Stir in coconut milk; cook an additional minute. Remove from heat; cool slightly. Puree in batches in a blender or food processor. If desired, top with minced fresh cilantro.
1 cup: 111 cal., 8g fat (5g sat. fat), 0 chol., 532mg sod., 10g carb. (4g sugars, 3g fiber), 3g pro.

★ ★ ★ ★ ★ **READER REVIEW**

"Really good flavor and easy. I only puree half of the soup because I personally like it better that way."
ROBYN TASTEOFHOME.COM

BUFFALO CHICKEN SLIDERS

BUFFALO CHICKEN SLIDERS

I came up with the idea for these slow-cooked sliders from my mom and dad, who'd made a similar version for a get-together. It's a versatile recipe; I sometimes serve different sauces and toppings on the side and let guests create their own slider.
—Christina Addison, Blanchester, OH

Prep: 20 min. • **Cook:** 3 hours
Makes: 6 servings

- 1 lb. boneless skinless chicken breasts
- 2 Tbsp. plus ⅓ cup Louisiana-style hot sauce, divided
- ¼ tsp. pepper
- ¼ cup butter, cubed
- ¼ cup honey
- 12 Hawaiian sweet rolls, warmed
  Optional ingredients: lettuce leaves, sliced tomato, thinly sliced red onion and crumbled blue cheese

1. Place chicken in a 3-qt. slow cooker. Toss with 2 Tbsp. hot sauce and pepper; cook, covered, on low until tender, for about 3-4 hours.
2. Remove chicken; discard the cooking juices. In a small saucepan, combine butter, honey and remaining hot sauce; cook and stir over medium heat until blended. Shred chicken with two forks; stir into sauce and heat through. Serve on Hawaiian sweet rolls with optional ingredients as desired.
Freeze option: Freeze cooled chicken mixture in freezer containers. To use, partially thaw in refrigerator overnight. Microwave chicken, covered, on high in a microwave-safe dish until heated through, stirring occasionally and adding a little water or broth if necessary.
2 sliders: 396 cal., 15g fat (8g sat. fat), 92mg chol., 873mg sod., 44g carb. (24g sugars, 2g fiber), 24g pro.

HAWAIIAN SAUSAGE SUBS

If you are looking for a different way to use kielbasa, look no further. The sweet, mildly spicy flavor of these bites makes a nice change of pace.
—Judy Dames, Bridgeville, PA

Prep: 15 min. • **Cook:** 3 hours
Makes: 12 servings

- 3 lbs. smoked kielbasa or Polish sausage, cut into 3-in. pieces
- 2 bottles (12 oz. each) chili sauce
- 1 can (20 oz.) pineapple tidbits, undrained
- ¼ cup packed brown sugar
- 12 hoagie buns, split
  Thinly sliced green onions, optional

Place kielbasa in a 3-qt. slow cooker. Combine the chili sauce, pineapple and brown sugar; pour over kielbasa. Cover and cook on low for 3-4 hours or until heated through. Serve sausage on buns. If desired, top with green onions.
1 sub: 663 cal., 35g fat (12g sat. fat), 76mg chol., 2532mg sod., 64g carb. (27g sugars, 1g fiber), 23g pro.

CUCUMBER SANDWICHES

I was introduced to a similar sandwich by a friend many years ago and then made my own version. Top them with thinly sliced onions for a pretty presentation.
—Karen Schriefer, Stevensville, MD

Takes: 15 min. • **Makes:** 6 servings

- 1 carton (8 oz.) spreadable cream cheese
- 2 tsp. ranch salad dressing mix
- 12 slices pumpernickel rye bread
- 2 to 3 medium cucumbers

In a large bowl, combine cream cheese and dressing mix. Spread on one side of each slice of bread. Peel cucumbers if desired; thinly slice and place on six slices of bread. Top with remaining bread. Serve immediately.
1 sandwich: 244cal., 10g fat (6g sat. fat), 24mg chol., 672mg sod., 31g carb. (3g sugars, 4g fiber), 8g pro.

HAWAIIAN SAUSAGE SUBS

PEPPERED PORK PITAS

PEPPERED PORK PITAS

Cracked black pepper and garlic give my quick and easy pork pitas some pop. Add some red peppers and garlic mayo (I like caramelized onions, too) to make your weeknight meals simply awesome.
—Katherine White, Henderson, NV

Takes: 20 min. • **Makes:** 4 servings

- 1 lb. boneless pork loin chops, cut into thin strips
- 1 Tbsp. olive oil
- 2 tsp. coarsely ground pepper
- 2 garlic cloves, minced
- 1 jar (12 oz.) roasted sweet red peppers, drained and julienned
- 4 whole pita breads, warmed Garlic mayonnaise and torn leaf lettuce, optional

In a small bowl, combine the pork, oil, pepper and garlic; toss to coat. Place a large skillet over medium-high heat. Add the pork mixture; cook and stir until no longer pink. Stir in red peppers; heat through. Serve on pita breads. Top with mayonnaise and lettuce if desired.

1 sandwich: 380 cal., 11g fat (3g sat. fat), 55mg chol., 665mg sod., 37g carb. (4g sugars, 2g fiber), 27g pro. **Diabetic exchanges:** 3 lean meat, 2 starch, 1 fat.

TEST KITCHEN TIP
Keep a jar of roasted sweet red peppers on hand. They add a quick and colorful touch to everything from sandwiches and scrambled eggs to casseroles and stir fries. Their mild yet familiar flavor makes them an easy addition to just about any dish.

**CHICKEN PESTO
WITH PASTA
PG 44**

Pizza & Pasta

When it comes to family favorites, nothing beats pizza and pasta. Casual, comforting, convenient—they'll keep everyone running to the table.

SHRIMP
TORTELLINI
PASTA TOSS

SHRIMP TORTELLINI PASTA TOSS

Meet your new go-to dish. This no-fuss skillet entree offers spring flavors with only a pinch of work. We loved way thyme and shrimp go together, but try the variations below as well.
—*Taste of Home* Test Kitchen

Takes: 20 min. • **Makes:** 4 servings

- 1 pkg. (9 oz.) refrigerated cheese tortellini
- 1 cup frozen peas
- 3 Tbsp. olive oil, divided
- 1 lb. uncooked shrimp (31-40 per lb.), peeled and deveined
- 2 garlic cloves, minced
- ¼ tsp. salt
- ¼ tsp. dried thyme
- ¼ tsp. pepper

1. Cook tortellini according to package directions, adding the peas during the last 5 minutes of cooking.
2. Meanwhile, in a large nonstick skillet, heat 2 Tbsp. oil over medium-high heat. Add shrimp; cook and stir 2 minutes. Add garlic; cook 1-2 minutes longer or until shrimp turn pink.
3. Drain tortellini mixture; add to skillet. Stir in salt, thyme, pepper and remaining oil; toss to coat.
1¼ cups: 413 cal., 17g fat (4g sat. fat), 165mg chol., 559mg sod., 36g carb. (4g sugars, 3g fiber), 29g pro. **Diabetic exchanges:** 4 lean meat, 2 starch, 2 fat.
Shrimp Asparagus Fettuccine Omit tortellini and peas. Bring 4 qt. water to a boil. Add 9 oz. refrigerated fettuccine and 1 cup cut fresh asparagus. Boil for 2-3 minutes or until pasta is tender. Proceed with the recipe as written but replace thyme with ¾ tsp. dried basil.
Soy Shrimp with Rice Noodles Omit tortellini and peas. Cook 8.8 oz. thin rice noodles according to package directions, adding 1 cup frozen shelled edamame during the last 4 minutes of cooking. Proceed with the recipe as written but replace the thyme with ¼ cup reduced-sodium soy sauce and omit salt.

BIG KAHUNA PIZZA

BIG KAHUNA PIZZA

A prebaked pizza crust and refrigerated barbecued pork make this tasty supper idea super fast and super easy. When cut into bite-sized pieces, it can double as a last-minute appetizer, too.
—Joni Hilton, Rocklin, CA

Takes: 30 min. • **Makes:** 6 servings

- 1 prebaked 12-in. pizza crust
- 1 carton (16 oz.) refrigerated fully cooked barbecued shredded pork
- 1 can (20 oz.) pineapple chunks, drained
- ⅓ cup chopped red onion
- 2 cups shredded part-skim mozzarella cheese

1. Preheat oven to 350°. Place pizza crust on an ungreased 12-in. pizza pan. Spread shredded pork over crust; top with the pineapple, onion and cheese.
2. Bake for 20-25 minutes or until cheese is melted.
1 slice: 443 cal., 12g fat (5g sat. fat), 45mg chol., 1133mg sod., 56g carb. (25g sugars, 2g fiber), 27g pro.

CLASSIC PESTO SAUCE

Homemade pesto just can't be beat. Serve it with any pasta of your choice.
—Sue Jurack, Mequon, WI

Takes: 15 min. • **Makes:** ½ cup

- ¾ cup loosely packed basil leaves
- 2 Tbsp. pine nuts or sunflower kernels
- 1 garlic clove, peeled
- ½ tsp. salt
- ⅛ tsp. pepper
- ⅓ cup olive oil
- ⅓ cup grated Parmesan cheese

Place the first five ingredients in a small food processor; pulse until chopped. Continue processing while gradually adding oil in a steady stream. Add cheese; pulse just until blended. Cover and freeze for up to 3 months. When freezing pesto, leave about ¾ in. of room on the top of the container, then cover the pesto with a thin layer of olive oil to keep it from turning brown during freezing.
2 Tbsp.: 217 cal., 22g fat (4g sat. fat), 5mg chol., 420mg sod., 1g carb. (0 sugars, 1g fiber), 4g pro.

CHORIZO PUMPKIN PASTA

CHORIZO PUMPKIN PASTA

I'm a busy student, and this spicy-sweet pasta makes a perfect quick dinner. Even better, it works on a bigger scale to feed a bunch of friends.
—Christine Yang, Syracuse, NY

Takes: 30 min. • **Makes:** 6 servings

- 3 cups uncooked gemelli or spiral pasta (about 12 oz.)
- 1 pkg. (12 oz.) fully cooked chorizo chicken sausage links or flavor of choice, sliced
- 1 cup canned pumpkin
- 1 cup half-and-half cream
- ¾ tsp. salt
- ¼ tsp. pepper
- 1½ cups shredded manchego or Monterey Jack cheese
  Minced fresh cilantro, optional

1. Cook pasta according to package directions. Drain, reserving ¾ cup of the pasta water.
2. Meanwhile, in a large skillet, saute sausage over medium heat until lightly browned; reduce heat to medium-low. Add pumpkin, cream, salt and pepper; cook and stir until heated through. Toss with pasta and enough pasta water to moisten; stir in cheese. If desired, sprinkle with cilantro.

1⅓ cups: 471 cal., 20g fat (11g sat. fat), 92mg chol., 847mg sod., 48g carb. (7g sugars, 3g fiber), 26g pro.

TEST KITCHEN TIP
Rely on canned pumpkin to add flair to dishes without much effort. Stir some into sloppy joe filling, spaghetti sauce, chili or even taco meat. It has a subtle earthy flavor that takes ho-hum dishes to heartwarming new heights.

CHEESY BOW TIE CHICKEN

Everyone we know loves warm, creamy spinach-artichoke dip, so adding it to pasta seemed like a natural fit.
—Sally Sibthorpe, Shelby Township, MI

Takes: 30 min. • **Makes:** 4 servings

- 2 pkg. (8 oz. each) frozen spinach and artichoke cheese dip
- 3 cups uncooked bow tie pasta
- 3 cups cubed rotisserie chicken
- 1 cup chopped roasted sweet red peppers
- ⅓ cup pitted Greek olives, halved
- ½ tsp. salt
- ¼ tsp. pepper

1. Heat cheese dip according to package directions. Meanwhile, in a Dutch oven, cook pasta according to the package directions; drain, reserving ½ cup pasta water. Return to pan.

2. Stir in chicken, cheese dip, peppers, olives, salt and pepper, adding enough reserved pasta water to achieve a creamy consistency; heat through.
1½ cups: 453 cal., 12 fat (3g sat. fat), 93mg chol., 795mg sod., 38g carb. (4g sugars, 2g fiber), 38g pro.

TEX-MEX PASTA

I wasn't able to stock up on groceries when I had surgery. After I got home, I looked at what was left in my pantry and created this. The results were fabulous.
—Michele Orthner, Lethbridge, AB

Takes: 30 min. • **Makes:** 4 servings

- 2 cups uncooked spiral pasta
- 1 lb. ground beef
- 1 jar (16 oz.) salsa
- 1 can (10¾ oz.) condensed cream of chicken soup, undiluted
- 1 cup shredded Mexican cheese blend, divided

1. Preheat oven to 350°. Cook pasta according to package directions.
2. Meanwhile, cook beef in a Dutch oven over medium heat until no longer pink; drain. Stir in the salsa, soup and ½ cup cheese; heat through.
3. Drain pasta; stir into meat mixture. Transfer to a greased 11x7-in. baking dish. Sprinkle with remaining cheese. Cover and bake 15-20 minutes or until cheese is melted.
1½ cups: 585 cal., 28 fat (11g sat. fat), 101mg chol., 1241mg sod., 46g carb. (6g sugars, 3g fiber), 33g pro.

SPINACH-ARTICHOKE RIGATONI

I love pasta, and so does my family. However, they are not so keen on their veggies. This one-pot meal gets us all eating our spinach.
—Yvonne Starlin, Westmoreland, TN

Takes: 30 min. • **Makes:** 4 servings

- 3 cups uncooked rigatoni or large tube pasta
- 1 pkg. (10 oz.) frozen creamed spinach
- 1 can (14 oz.) water-packed artichoke hearts, rinsed, drained and quartered
- 2 cups shredded part-skim mozzarella cheese, divided
- ¼ cup grated Parmesan cheese
- ½ tsp. salt
- ¼ tsp. pepper

1. Preheat broiler. Prepare rigatoni and spinach according to package directions.
2. Drain pasta, reserving ½ cup pasta water; return to pan. Add the artichoke hearts, ½ cup mozzarella cheese, Parmesan cheese, salt, pepper and creamed spinach; toss to combine, adding some of the reserved pasta water to thin, if desired.
3. Transfer to a greased 2-qt. broiler-safe baking dish; sprinkle with remaining mozzarella cheese. Broil 4-6 in. from heat 2-3 minutes or until cheese is melted.
1½ cups: 448 cal., 14g fat (8g sat. fat), 37mg chol., 1224mg sod., 54g carb. (6g sugars, 3g fiber), 28g pro.

CHEESY BOW TIE CHICKEN

EASY STUFFED SHELLS

EASY STUFFED SHELLS

I created a super easy way to fill pasta shells—just use packaged meatballs. Put the kids on stuffing duty. They'll be proud to help, and they'll rush to the table when it's time to eat.

—Dolores Betchner, Cudahy, WI

Prep: 20 min. • **Bake:** 40 min.
Makes: 12 servings

- 36 uncooked jumbo pasta shells
- 1 jar (24 oz.) spaghetti sauce
- 36 frozen fully cooked Italian meatballs (½ oz. each), thawed
- 2 cups shredded part-skim mozzarella cheese

1. Preheat oven to 350°. Cook pasta shells according to package directions; drain and rinse in cold water.
2. Spread ½ cup sauce into a greased 13x9-in. baking dish. Fill each shell with a meatball; place over sauce. Top with the remaining sauce and the cheese.
3. Bake, covered, 35 minutes. Uncover; bake 3-5 minutes longer or until bubbly and cheese is melted.

3 stuffed shells: 334 cal., 17g fat (8g sat. fat), 45mg chol., 711mg sod., 30g carb. (6g sugars, 3g fiber), 16g pro.

TOMATO-BASIL PITA PIZZAS

This is one of my favorite warm-weather recipes. It's so quick and tasty! You can use it as a snack, appetizer or entree. Double or triple it to suit your needs.

—Barbra Annino, Galena, IL

Takes: 20 min. • **Makes:** 2 servings

- 2 pita breads (6 in.)
- 2 plum tomatoes, thinly sliced
- 8 fresh basil leaves, thinly sliced
- ¼ cup shredded Asiago cheese
- 2 tsp. olive oil

Preheat oven to 350°. Place pita breads on an ungreased baking sheet. Layer with tomatoes, basil and cheese; drizzle with the oil. Bake for 12-14 minutes or until cheese is melted.

1 pizza: 269 cal., 9g fat (3g sat. fat), 12mg chol., 362mg sod., 37g carb. (3g sugars, 2g fiber), 10g pro. **Diabetic exchanges:** 2 starch, 1 lean meat, 1 vegetable, 1 fat.

Family Classic

RAVIOLI WITH APPLE CHICKEN SAUSAGE

RAVIOLI WITH APPLE CHICKEN SAUSAGE

I love butternut squash ravioli but was never quite sure what flavors would best complement the squash. Turns out that creamy spinach, chicken sausage and a hint of sweet spice are the perfect additions. Yum!
—Mary Brodeur, Millbury, MA

Takes: 30 min. • **Makes:** 4 servings

1 pkg. (18 oz.) frozen butternut squash ravioli
2 pkg. (10 oz. each) frozen creamed spinach
1 Tbsp. olive oil
1 pkg. (12 oz.) fully cooked apple chicken sausage links or flavor of your choice, cut into ½-in. slices
1 tsp. maple syrup
¼ tsp. pumpkin pie spice

1. Cook ravioli according to package directions. Prepare spinach according to package directions. Meanwhile, in a large skillet, heat oil over medium heat. Add sausage; cook and stir for 2-4 minutes or until browned.
2. Drain ravioli. Add ravioli, spinach, maple syrup and pie spice to sausage; heat through.
1½ cups: 622 cal., 20g fat (6g sat. fat), 64mg chol., 2098mg sod., 81g carb. (25g sugars, 6g fiber), 30g pro.

SPAGHETTI WITH EGGS & BACON

Most people are surprised to see this combination of ingredients. Then they taste it—and it's gone in a flash.
—Gail Jenner, Etna, CA

Takes: 25 min. • **Makes:** 4 servings

8 oz. uncooked spaghetti
4 large eggs
¾ cup half-and-half cream
½ cup grated Parmesan cheese
½ lb. bacon strips, cooked and crumbled
Additional grated Parmesan cheese, optional

1. Cook spaghetti according to package directions in a 6-qt. stockpot. In a small saucepan, whisk eggs and cream until blended. Cook over low heat until a thermometer reads 160°, stirring the mixture constantly (do not allow to simmer). Remove from heat; stir in Parmesan cheese.
2. Drain spaghetti; return to stockpot. Add sauce and bacon; toss to combine. Serve immediately. If desired, sprinkle with additional cheese.
1 serving: 486 cal., 21g fat (9g sat. fat), 238mg chol., 611mg sod., 45g carb. (3g sugars, 2g fiber), 26g pro.

drain and set aside. In the same pan, cook sausage over medium heat 5-6 minutes or until browned.

2. Stir in the spaghetti sauce, salsa and reserved beef; heat through. Serve with the pasta.

1 cup: 325 cal., 21g fat (7g sat. fat), 60mg chol., 1378mg sod., 18g carb. (11g sugars, 2g fiber), 17g pro.

ARTICHOKE BLUE CHEESE FETTUCCINE

When I'm in a rush, I use store-bought Alfredo sauce to speed along my blue-cheesy noodles with mushrooms. Fresh refrigerated fettuccine gets done even faster than the dried variety.
—Jolanthe Erb, Harrisonburg, VA

Takes: 20 min. • **Makes:** 4 servings

- 1   pkg. (12 oz.) fettuccine
- 1   cup sliced fresh mushrooms
- 1   can (14 oz.) water-packed artichoke hearts, drained and chopped
- 1½ cups Alfredo sauce
- ¼   cup crumbled blue cheese

1. Cook fettuccine according to package directions.

2. Meanwhile, place a large nonstick skillet coated with cooking spray over medium-high heat. Add mushrooms and artichoke hearts; cook and stir until mushrooms are tender. Stir in Alfredo sauce; bring to a boil over medium heat. Reduce heat; simmer, uncovered, 5 minutes, stirring mixture occasionally.

3. Drain fettuccine, reserving ⅓ cup pasta water. Add fettuccine to the artichoke mixture; toss to combine, adding some reserved pasta water to thin if desired. Sprinkle with blue cheese.

1 cup: 499 cal., 14g fat (9g sat. fat), 33mg chol., 770mg sod., 74g carb. (6g sugars, 4g fiber), 21g pro.

TEST KITCHEN TIP
Fresh mushrooms add great flavor to pasta dishes and pizza; however, if you're a cook who's often pressed for time, stash a few cans of mushrooms in the pantry. You can use them to replace fresh mushrooms in many entrees.

BACON & SPINACH PIZZA

BACON & SPINACH PIZZA

Our go-to pizza is a snap to make using packaged pizza crust and ready-to-serve bacon. The kids don't even mind the spinach on top.
—Annette Riva, Naperville, IL

Start to Finish: 20 min.
Makes: 6 servings

- 1   prebaked 12-inch pizza crust
- ⅓   cup pizza sauce
- 1   cup shaved Parmesan cheese
- 2   cups fresh baby spinach, thinly sliced
- 8   ready-to-serve fully cooked bacon strips, cut into 1-inch pieces

Preheat oven to 450°. Place crust on an ungreased baking sheet. Spread with sauce; top with ½ cup cheese, spinach and bacon. Sprinkle with remaining cheese. Bake until cheese is melted, 8-10 minutes.

1 slice: 269 cal., 10g fat (4g sat. fat), 10mg chol., 726mg sod., 31g carb. (2g sugars, 2g fiber), 15g pro.

SUPER SPAGHETTI SAUCE

At my house, we never know how many we'll have for dinner. That's why this spaghetti sauce is one of my favorites— flavorful, filling and fast. Smoked kielbasa gives it depth, and salsa adds the kick.
—Bella Anderson, Chester, SC

Takes: 30 min. • **Makes:** 2½ qt.

- 1   lb. ground beef
- 1   lb. smoked kielbasa, cut into ¼-in. slices
- 2   jars (24 oz. each) spaghetti sauce with mushrooms
- 1   jar (16 oz.) chunky salsa
      Hot cooked pasta

1. In a Dutch oven, cook ground beef over medium heat until no longer pink;

BUCATINI WITH
SAUSAGE & KALE

BUCATINI WITH
SAUSAGE & KALE

*I was short on time, but I
wanted to make an elegant
dinner for my husband
and me. That night, we ate
this simple pasta starring
spicy sausage and our homegrown kale.*
—Angela Lemoine, Howell, NJ

Takes: 30 min. • **Makes:** 6 servings

1   pkg. (12 oz.) bucatini pasta
    or fettuccine
2   tsp. plus 3 Tbsp. olive oil, divided

1   lb. regular or spicy bulk Italian
    sausage
5   garlic cloves, thinly sliced
8   cups chopped fresh kale
    (about 5 oz.)
¾   tsp. salt
¼   tsp. pepper
    Shredded Romano cheese

1. Cook pasta according to the package
directions, decreasing time by 3 minutes.
Drain, reserving 2 cups pasta water. Toss
pasta with 2 tsp. oil.
2. In a 6-qt. stockpot, cook sausage over
medium heat until no longer pink, about

5-7 minutes, breaking sausage into large
crumbles. Add garlic and remaining oil;
cook and stir 2 minutes. Stir in kale, salt
and pepper; cook, covered, over
medium-low heat until kale is tender,
about 10 minutes, stirring occasionally.
3. Add pasta and reserved pasta water;
bring to a boil. Reduce heat; simmer,
uncovered, until pasta is al dente and
liquid is absorbed, about 3 minutes,
tossing to combine. Sprinkle with cheese.
1⅓ cups: 512 cal., 30g fat (8g sat. fat),
51mg chol., 898mg sod., 43g carb. (2g
sugars, 3g fiber), 19g pro.

CHICKEN PESTO WITH PASTA

Keep a container of pesto on hand. The next time you have leftover chicken, whip up this simple pasta for lunch or dinner.
—*Taste of Home* Test Kitchen

Takes: 20 min. • **Makes:** 8 servings

- 1 pkg. (16 oz.) cellentani or spiral pasta
- 2 cups cubed rotisserie chicken
- 2 medium tomatoes, chopped
- 1 container (7 oz.) prepared pesto
- ¼ cup pine nuts, toasted

In a Dutch oven, cook pasta according to package directions; drain and return to pan. Stir in chicken, tomatoes and pesto; heat through. Sprinkle with pine nuts.
Note: To toast nuts, bake in a shallow pan in a 350° oven for 5-10 minutes or cook in a skillet over low heat until nuts are lightly browned, stirring occasionally.
1¼ cups: 433 cal., 18g fat (5g sat. fat), 40mg chol., 239mg sod., 45g carb. (3g sugars, 3g fiber), 24g pro.

BARBECUED CHICKEN PIZZA

Barbecue sauce is a surprising flavor change when you need a quick pizza sauce for a hectic night's dinner. Ham works just as well as chicken here.
—Patricia Richardson, Verona, ON

Takes: 20 min. • **Makes:** 4 servings

- 1 prebaked 12-in. pizza crust
- ⅔ cup honey garlic barbecue sauce
- 1 small red onion, chopped
- 1 cup cubed cooked chicken
- 2 cups shredded part-skim mozzarella cheese

Preheat oven to 350°. Place the crust on a 14-in. pizza pan. Spread barbecue sauce to within ½ in. of edges. Sprinkle with the onion, chicken and cheese. Bake pizza for 10 minutes or until cheese is melted.
1 slice: 510 cal., 18g fat (7g sat. fat), 64mg chol., 1158mg sod., 52g carb. (7g sugars, 1g fiber), 35g pro.

CHICKEN PESTO WITH PASTA

LUNCH BOX PIZZAS

It's no challenge to find a lunch the kids will eat when you have these. Plus they pack nicely and travel well.
—Rhonda Cliett, Belton, TX

Takes: 20 min. • **Makes:** 10 servings

- 1 tube (7½ oz.) refrigerated buttermilk biscuits (10 biscuits)
- ¼ cup tomato sauce
- 1 tsp. Italian seasoning
- 10 slices pepperoni
- ¾ cup shredded Monterey Jack cheese

Preheat the oven to 425°. Flatten each biscuit into a 3-in. circle; press into a greased muffin cup. Combine tomato sauce and Italian seasoning; spoon 1 teaspoonful into each; top with 1 slice of pepperoni and about 1 Tbsp. of cheese.

Bake for 10-15 minutes or until golden brown. Serve pizzas immediately or store in the refrigerator.

1 pizza: 94 cal., 4g fat (2g sat. fat), 9mg chol., 292mg sod., 11g carb. (0 sugars, 0 fiber), 4g pro.

PEPPERED PORTOBELLO PENNE

The hearty mushrooms mean you won't miss the meat, and a kickin' hot cheese sauce takes this simple pasta toss from drab to fab. My family thinks it tastes just like a restaurant dish.
—Veronica Callaghan, Glastonbury, CT

Takes: 30 min. • **Makes:** 4 servings

- 2 cups uncooked penne pasta
- 4 large portobello mushrooms, stems removed, halved and thinly sliced

LUNCH BOX PIZZAS

- 2 Tbsp. olive oil
- ½ cup heavy whipping cream
- ¾ tsp. salt
- ¼ tsp. pepper
- 1 cup shredded pepper jack cheese

1. Cook pasta according to package directions.

2. Meanwhile, in a large skillet, saute mushrooms in oil until tender. Stir in the cream, salt and pepper; heat through. Stir in cheese until melted. Drain pasta. Add to skillet and toss to coat.

1 cup: 503 cal., 28g fat (13g sat. fat), 71mg chol., 632mg sod., 48g carb. (3g sugars, 3g fiber), 17g pro.

SAUSAGE MANICOTTI

This familiar Italian-style entree comes together in a snap. It's a comforting dish that says "home" to my family and is easy to freeze and have on hand.
—Carolyn Henderson, Maple Plain, MN

Prep: 15 min.
Bake: 65 min.
Makes: 7 servings

- 1 lb. uncooked bulk pork sausage
- 2 cups 4% cottage cheese
- 1 pkg. (8 oz.) manicotti shells
- 1 jar (24 oz.) marinara sauce
- 1 cup shredded part-skim mozzarella cheese

1. Preheat oven to 350°. In a large bowl, combine sausage and cottage cheese. Stuff into the uncooked manicotti shells. Place in a greased 13x9-in. baking dish. Top manicotti with the marinara sauce.

2. Cover and bake for 55-60 minutes or until a thermometer inserted into the center of a shell reads 160°.

3. Uncover; sprinkle with the mozzarella cheese. Bake 8-10 minutes longer or until cheese is melted. Let stand for 5 minutes before serving.

Freeze option: Transfer individual portions of cooled manicotti to freezer containers; freeze. To use, partially thaw in refrigerator overnight. Transfer to a microwave-safe dish and microwave on high, stirring occasionally and adding a little spaghetti sauce if necessary.

2 manicotti: 489 cal., 24g fat (10g sat. fat), 59mg chol., 1232mg sod., 41g carb. (12g sugars, 3g fiber), 27g pro.

WEEKNIGHT LASAGNA

Four-ingredient lasagna? It sounds too good to be true, but this mouthwatering entree proves it's possible. While my husband and I really love lasagna, it's so time-consuming to assemble that I rarely made it until I discovered this clever way of using frozen ravioli to cut the prep time down to minutes.

—Pamela Nicholson, Festus, MO

Prep: 15 min. • **Bake:** 45 min.
Makes: 6 servings

- 1   jar (24 oz.) pasta sauce
- 1   pkg. (25 oz.) frozen meat or cheese ravioli
- 3   cups fresh baby spinach
- 1½ cups shredded part-skim mozzarella cheese

1. Preheat the oven to 350°. In a small saucepan, heat sauce 5-7 minutes over medium heat or just until simmering, stirring occasionally.
2. Spread ½ cup sauce into a greased 11x7-in. baking dish. Layer with half of the ravioli, 1½ cups spinach, ½ cup cheese and half of the remaining sauce; repeat layers. Sprinkle with the remaining mozzarella cheese.
3. Bake, uncovered, 45-50 minutes or until the edges are bubbly and the cheese is melted. Let lasagna stand 5 minutes before serving.
1 cup: 344 cal., 10g fat (5g sat. fat), 26mg chol., 850mg sod., 45g carb. (10g sugars, 5g fiber), 17g pro. **Diabetic exchanges:** 3 starch, 2 medium-fat meat.

TORTELLINI CARBONARA

Bacon, cream and Parmesan cheese make a classic pasta sauce that's absolutely heavenly. It's a great option for company!
—Cathy Croyle, Davidsville, PA

Takes: 20 min. • **Makes:** 4 servings

- 1   pkg. (9 oz.) refrigerated cheese tortellini
- 8   bacon strips, chopped
- 1   cup heavy whipping cream
- ½   cup grated Parmesan cheese
- ½   cup chopped fresh parsley

1. Cook tortellini according to package directions; drain.
2. Meanwhile, in a large skillet, cook bacon over medium heat until crisp, stirring occasionally. Remove with a slotted spoon; drain on paper towels. Pour off drippings.
3. In same pan, combine cream, cheese, parsley and bacon; heat through over medium heat. Stir in the tortellini. Serve immediately.
1 cup: 527 cal., 36g fat (20g sat. fat), 121mg chol., 728mg sod., 33g carb. (3g sugars, 2g fiber), 19g pro.

✳

TEST KITCHEN TIP

Traditional carbonara sauce usually involves eggs. If you'd like to go the traditional route, try cutting the cream in this recipe in half and tempering two whisked eggs into the sauce. Temper your eggs by adding a small amount of the hot cream mixture to the whisked eggs and whisking them together some more before adding the mixture back to the pan. This preserves the creamy texture. Be sure to take the pan off the heat to keep the eggs from scrambling.

WEEKNIGHT LASAGNA

Family Classic

SAVORY
PORK ROAST
PG 50

Beef & Pork

Hearty meals don't have to steal all your free time.
Sink your teeth in to these mouthwatering entrees
that come together without a hitch.

SAVORY PORK ROAST

(PICTURED ON PG 48)

I love this herbed roast so much that I make it as often as I can. It's amazing what garlic and sage can do for pork, and this entree is wonderful for special occasions, particularly when served alongside sweet potatoes and buttery corn muffins.
—Edie DeSpain, Logan, UT

Prep: 5 min. • **Bake:** 80 min. + standing
Makes: 12 servings

- 1 garlic clove, minced
- 2 tsp. dried marjoram
- 1 tsp. salt
- 1 tsp. rubbed sage
- 1 boneless whole pork
     loin roast (4 lbs.)

1. Preheat oven to 350°. Combine the seasonings; rub over roast. Place roast on a rack in a shallow roasting pan.
2. Bake, uncovered, for 80 minutes or until a thermometer reads 145°. Let stand for 10-15 minutes before slicing.
4 oz. cooked pork: 188 cal., 7g fat (3g sat. fat), 75mg chol., 240mg sod., 0 carb. (0 sugars, 0 fiber), 29g pro. **Diabetic exchanges:** 4 lean meat.

LOADED FLANK STEAK

I wanted to do something a little different with flank steak, so I stuffed it with bacon, green onions and ranch dressing.
—Tammy Thomas, Mustang, OK

Takes: 25 min. • **Makes:** 6 servings

- ½ cup butter, softened
- 6 bacon strips, cooked and crumbled
- 3 green onions, chopped
- 2 Tbsp. ranch salad dressing mix
- ½ tsp. pepper
- 1 beef flank steak (1½ to 2 lbs.)

1. In a small bowl, beat the first five ingredients. Cut a pocket horizontally in steak; fill with butter mixture.
2. Grill steak, covered, over medium heat or broil 4 in. from heat 5-7 minutes on each side or until meat reaches desired doneness (for medium-rare, a thermometer should read 135°; medium, 140°; medium-well, 145°). Let stand 5 minutes before serving. To serve, slice across the grain.

4 oz. cooked beef: 267 cal., 20g fat (10g sat. fat), 76mg chol., 714mg sod., 4g carb. (0 sugars, 0 fiber), 18g pro.

BBQ MEAT LOAF MINIS

Kids can have fun helping prepare these mini meat loaves in muffin cups. If we're in the mood for extra spice, we just add 2 teaspoons chili powder and 1 cup of salsa.
—Linda Call, Falun, KS

Takes: 30 min. • **Makes:** 6 servings

- 1 pkg. (6 oz.) stuffing mix
- 1 cup water
- 2 Tbsp. hickory smoke-flavored
     barbecue sauce
- 1 lb. ground beef
- 1 cup shredded cheddar cheese
     Additional hickory smoke-flavored
     barbecue sauce, optional

1. Preheat oven to 375°. In a large bowl, combine stuffing mix, water and 2 Tbsp. barbecue sauce. Add beef; mix lightly but thoroughly. Press ⅓ cup of mixture into each of 12 ungreased muffin cups.
2. Bake, uncovered, for 18-22 minutes or until a thermometer reads 160°. Sprinkle the tops with cheese; bake 2-4 minutes longer or until the cheese is melted. If desired, serve meat loaves with additional barbecue sauce.
Freeze option: Cover and freeze cooled meat loaves on a plastic wrap-lined baking sheet until firm. Transfer meat loaves to a resealable plastic freezer bag; return to freezer. To use, partially thaw loaves in refrigerator overnight. Place meat loaves on a greased shallow baking pan. Bake in a preheated 350° oven until heated through. Top with cheese as directed.
2 mini meat loaves: 330 cal., 17g fat (7g sat. fat), 67mg chol., 668mg sod., 21g carb. (4g sugars, 1g fiber), 21g pro.

BBQ MEAT LOAF MINIS

ASIAN BEEF & NOODLES

This yummy, economical dish takes only a few ingredients—all of which are easy to keep on hand. Serve with a dash of soy sauce and a side of fresh pineapple slices. You can also try it with ground turkey instead of beef!
—Laura Stenberg, WY, MN

Takes: 20 min. • **Makes:** 4 servings

- 1 lb. lean ground beef (90% lean)
- 2 pkg. (3 oz. each) Oriental ramen noodles, crumbled
- 2½ cups water
- 2 cups frozen broccoli stir-fry vegetable blend
- ¼ tsp. ground ginger
- 2 Tbsp. thinly sliced green onion

1. In a large skillet, cook the beef over medium heat until no longer pink; drain. Add the contents of one ramen noodle flavoring packet; stir until dissolved. Remove beef and set aside.

2. In the same skillet, combine the water, vegetables, ginger, noodles and contents of remaining flavoring packet. Bring to a boil. Reduce heat; cover and simmer for 3-4 minutes or until noodles are tender, stirring occasionally. Return beef to the pan and heat through. Stir in onion.

1½ cups: 377 cal., 15g fat (7g sat. fat), 56mg chol., 624mg sod., 31g carb. (3g sugars, 3g fiber), 27g pro. **Diabetic exchanges:** 3 lean meat, 2 starch, 1 fat.

DID YOU KNOW?
Frozen veggies are usually flash frozen at their peak, which means you are receiving the best nutrients they have to offer.

ASIAN BEEF & NOODLES

SLOW COOKER KALUA PORK & CABBAGE

PLUM-GLAZED COUNTRY RIBS

When planning to make ribs one day, I remembered that a friend had given me homemade plum jelly. I stirred some into the sauce for a pleasant fruity accent.
—Ila Mae Alderman, Galax, VA

Prep: 5 min. • **Bake:** 1¼ hours
Makes: 8 servings

- 4   to 4½ lbs. bone-in country-style pork ribs
- 1   bottle (12 oz.) chili sauce
- 1   jar (12 to 13 oz.) plum preserves or preserves of your choice
- ¼   cup soy sauce
- ¼   tsp. hot pepper sauce

1. Preheat oven to 350°. Place ribs in two ungreased 13x9-in. baking dishes. Bake, uncovered, for 45 minutes; drain.
2. In a small saucepan, combine the remaining ingredients. Bring to a boil, stirring occasionally. Remove from the heat. Set aside ¾ cup sauce for serving.
3. Brush ribs with some of the remaining sauce. Bake, uncovered, about 30-45 minutes or until ribs are tender, turning and basting frequently with remaining sauce. Serve with reserved sauce.
8 oz. cooked pork: 391 cal., 14g fat (5g sat. fat), 86mg chol., 1214mg sod., 40g carb. (35g sugars, 0 fiber), 27g pro.

SLOW COOKER KALUA PORK & CABBAGE

My slow-cooked pork has four ingredients and takes less than 10 minutes to prep. The result tastes just like the Kalua pork made in Hawaii that's slow roasted all day in an underground oven.
—Rholinelle DeTorres, San Jose, CA

Prep: 10 min. • **Cook:** 9 hours
Makes: 12 servings

- 7   bacon strips, divided
- 1   boneless pork shoulder butt roast (3 to 4 lbs.), well trimmed
- 1   Tbsp. coarse sea salt
- 1   medium head cabbage (about 2 lbs.), coarsely chopped

1. Line bottom of a 6-qt. slow cooker with four bacon strips. Sprinkle all sides of the roast with salt; place in a slow cooker. Arrange remaining bacon over the top of the roast.
2. Cook, covered, on low 8-10 hours or until pork is tender. Add the cabbage, spreading cabbage around roast. Cook, covered, 1 to 1¼ hours longer or until cabbage is tender.
3. Remove pork to a serving bowl; shred pork with two forks. Using a slotted spoon, add cabbage to pork and toss to combine. If desired, skim fat from some of the cooking juices; stir juices into pork mixture or serve on the side.
1 cup: 227 cal., 13g fat (5g sat. fat), 72mg chol., 622mg sod., 4g carb. (2g sugars, 2g fiber), 22g pro.

Family Classic

**PLUM-GLAZED
COUNTRY RIBS**

HAM & SWISS STROMBOLI

This is a treat to take to a potluck or to surprise someone with dinner. It's also easy to change up the recipe with any of your favorite meats or cheeses.

—Tricia Bibb, Hartselle, AL

Takes: 30 min. • **Makes:** 6 servings

- 1 tube (11 oz.) refrigerated crusty French loaf
- 6 oz. sliced deli ham
- ¼ cup finely chopped onion
- 8 bacon strips, cooked and crumbled
- 6 oz. sliced Swiss cheese
  Honey mustard, optional

1. Preheat oven to 375°. Unroll dough on a baking sheet. Place ham down center third of dough to within 1 in. of ends; top with onion, bacon and cheese. Fold long sides of dough over filling, pinching seam and ends to seal; tuck ends under. Cut several slits in top.

2. Bake 20-25 minutes or until golden brown. Cut into slices. If desired, serve with honey mustard.

Freeze option: Securely wrap and freeze cooled unsliced stromboli in heavy-duty foil. To use, reheat the stromboli on an ungreased baking sheet in a preheated 375° oven until heated through and a thermometer inserted in the center of the stromboli reads 165°.

1 slice: 272 cal., 11g fat (5g sat. fat), 40mg chol., 795mg sod., 26g carb. (3g sugars, 1g fiber), 18g pro.

BRISKET WITH CRANBERRY GRAVY

Cranberry sauce adds pleasant sweetness and rich color to this dish. You can also use jellied sauce instead of whole berry sauce if you prefer.

—Nina Hall, Spokane, WA

Prep: 25 min. • **Cook:** 8 hours
Makes: 8 servings

- 1 fresh beef brisket (2½ lbs.)
- ½ tsp. salt
- ¼ tsp. pepper
- 1 can (14 oz.) whole-berry cranberry sauce
- 1 can (8 oz.) tomato sauce
- ½ cup chopped onion
- 1 Tbsp. prepared mustard

1. Rub brisket with salt and pepper; place in a 5-qt. slow cooker. Combine the cranberry sauce, tomato sauce, onion and mustard; pour over brisket.

2. Cover and cook on low for 8-10 hours or until meat is tender. Remove brisket; thinly slice across the grain. Skim fat from cooking juices; serve juices with brisket.

Note: This is a fresh beef brisket, not corned beef.

4 oz. cooked brisket: 262 cal., 6g fat (2g sat. fat), 60mg chol., 357mg sod., 21g carb. (13g sugars, 1g fiber), 30g pro.

Diabetic exchanges: 4 lean meat, 1 starch.

SMOTHERED BURRITOS

My brother-in-law once teased that I knew how to cook only five things using ground beef. I had to prove him wrong, so I came up with these burritos.
—Kim Kenyon, Greenwood, MO

Takes: 25 min. • **Makes:** 4 servings

- 1 can (10 oz.) green enchilada sauce
- ¾ cup salsa verde
- 1 lb. ground beef
- 4 flour tortillas (10 in.)
- 1½ cups shredded cheddar cheese, divided

1. Preheat oven to 375°. In a small bowl, mix enchilada sauce and salsa verde.
2. In a large skillet, cook the beef over medium heat 8-10 minutes or until no longer pink, breaking into crumbles; drain. Stir in ½ cup sauce mixture.
3. Spoon ⅔ cup beef mixture across the center of each tortilla; top each with 3 Tbsp. cheese. Fold bottom and sides of tortilla over filling and roll up.
4. Place in a greased 11x7-in. baking dish. Pour remaining sauce mixture over top; sprinkle with remaining ¾ cup cheese. Bake, uncovered, 10-15 minutes or until cheese is melted.

1 burrito: 624 cal., 33g fat (15g sat. fat), 115mg chol., 1470mg sod., 44g carb. (6g sugars, 2g fiber), 36g pro.

SKILLET BEEF & POTATOES

Sirloin strips with red potatoes and fresh rosemary are seriously amazing and ready in a flash. The key is precooking potatoes in the microwave to speed the process.
—*Taste of Home* Test Kitchen

Takes: 25 min. • **Makes:** 4 servings

- 1½ lbs. red potatoes (about 5 medium), halved and cut into ¼-in. slices
- ⅓ cup water
- ½ tsp. salt
- 1 lb. beef top sirloin steak, cut into thin strips
- ½ cup chopped onion
- 3 Tbsp. olive oil, divided
- 2 tsp. garlic pepper blend
- 1½ tsp. minced fresh rosemary

1. Place potatoes, water and salt in a microwave-safe dish; microwave, covered, on high until potatoes are tender, 7-9 minutes. Drain.
2. Meanwhile, toss the beef with the onion, 2 Tbsp. oil and pepper blend. Place a large skillet over medium-high heat. Add half of the beef mixture; cook and stir until beef is browned, about 1-2 minutes. Remove from pan; repeat with remaining beef mixture.
3. In a clean skillet, heat remaining oil over medium-high heat. Add potatoes; cook the potatoes until lightly browned, about 4-5 minutes, turning occasionally. Stir in beef mixture; heat through. Sprinkle with the rosemary.

1½ cups: 320 cal., 16g fat (4g sat. fat), 63mg chol., 487mg sod., 20g carb. (2g sugars, 2g fiber), 23g pro. **Diabetic exchanges:** 3 lean meat, 2 fat, 1 starch.

SMOTHERED BURRITOS

MEXICAN STUFFED PEPPERS

This economical summer meal makes the most of my homegrown peppers. I like to top the peppers with cool sour cream and serve tortilla chips and salsa alongside.
—Kim Coleman, Columbia, SC

Prep: 25 min. • **Bake:** 30 min.
Makes: 8 servings

- 1 lb. lean ground beef (90% lean)
- 1 can (14½ oz.) diced tomatoes and green chilies, undrained
- 1 envelope (5.4 oz.) Mexican-style rice and pasta mix
- 1½ cups water
- 8 medium sweet peppers
- 2 cups shredded Mexican cheese blend, divided

1. Preheat oven to 375°. In a large skillet, cook and crumble beef over medium heat until no longer pink, 5-7 minutes; drain. Stir in the tomatoes, rice mix and water; bring to a boil. Reduce the heat; simmer, covered, until liquid is absorbed, 6-8 minutes.

2. Cut and discard tops from peppers; remove seeds. Place peppers in a greased 13x9-in. baking dish. Place ⅓ cup beef mixture in each pepper; sprinkle each with 2 Tbsp. cheese. Top with remaining rice mixture. Bake, covered, 25 minutes.

3. Sprinkle with remaining cheese. Bake, uncovered, until cheese is melted and peppers are crisp-tender, 5-10 minutes.

1 stuffed pepper: 301 cal., 14g fat (8g sat. fat), 61mg chol., 797mg sod., 23g carb. (4g sugars, 3g fiber), 20g pro.

MEXICAN STUFFED PEPPERS

PEACHY PORK WITH RICE

PEACHY PORK WITH RICE

Tender pork tenderloin does a fabulous job of showing off my homemade peach preserves. Tweak the heat level by using mild or spicy salsa and seasonings.
—Melissa Molaison, Hawkinsville, GA

Takes: 30 min. • **Makes:** 4 servings

1½ cups uncooked instant brown rice
1 pork tenderloin (1 lb.), cut into 1-in. cubes
2 Tbsp. olive oil
2 Tbsp. reduced-sodium taco seasoning
1 cup salsa
3 Tbsp. peach preserves

1. Cook rice according to the package directions. Meanwhile, place pork in a large bowl; drizzle with oil. Sprinkle with taco seasoning; toss to coat.
2. Place a large nonstick skillet coated with cooking spray over medium heat. Add pork; cook and stir 8-10 minutes or until no longer pink. Stir in salsa and preserves; heat through. Serve with rice.
1 cup pork with ½ cup rice: 387 cal., 12g fat (2g sat. fat), 63mg chol., 540mg sod., 42g carb. (13g sugars, 2g fiber), 25g pro. **Diabetic exchanges:** 3 lean meat, 2½ starch, 1½ fat.

RYE BREAD-TOPPED REUBEN CASSEROLE

Not only delicious, it's easier to eat than the sandwich version at potluck dinners.
—Nita White, Cedar Springs, MI

Takes: 30 min. • **Makes:** 4 servings

1 can (14 oz.) sauerkraut, rinsed and well drained
1 cup Thousand Island salad dressing
1 lb. thinly sliced deli corned beef, cut into strips
2 cups shredded Swiss cheese
4 to 6 slices rye bread, buttered

1. Preheat oven to 375°. In a large bowl, combine sauerkraut and salad dressing; spread into a greased 13x9-in. baking dish. Top with corned beef and cheese.
2. Place bread, buttered side up, over the top. Bake, uncovered, for 25-30 minutes or until the Reuben casserole is heated through and bubbly.
1 cup: 705 cal., 44g fat (16g sat. fat), 143mg chol., 3149mg sod., 33g carb. (13g sugars, 5g fiber), 41g pro.

**BASIL
PORK CHOPS**

BASIL PORK CHOPS

These tender, glazed chops get a kick of flavor from basil, chili powder and a little brown sugar. Serve with your favorite roasted veggies and you've got a super comforting meal bursting with flavor.
—Lisa Gilliland, Fort Collins, CO

Takes: 25 min. • **Makes:** 4 servings

- ¼ cup packed brown sugar
- 1½ tsp. dried basil
- ½ tsp. salt
- ½ tsp. chili powder
- 2 Tbsp. canola oil, divided
- 4 boneless pork loin chops
  (½ in. thick and 4 oz. each)

1. Mix first four ingredients; gradually stir in 1 Tbsp. oil (mixture will be crumbly). Rub over both sides of pork chops.
2. In a large skillet, heat the remaining oil over medium heat; cook chops until a thermometer reads 145°, 4-6 minutes per side. Let pork chops stand 5 minutes before serving.
1 pork chop: 152 cal., 8g fat (1g sat. fat), 14mg chol., 312mg sod., 14g carb. (13g sugars, 0 fiber), 6g pro.

BEEF TIPS WITH HORSERADISH GRAVY

It takes only 25 minutes to put this impressive dinner on the table for your family or company.
—Laura Majchrzak, Hunt Valley, MD

Takes: 25 min. • **Makes:** 4 servings

- 1 pkg. (17 oz.) refrigerated beef tips with gravy
- 1 cup creme fraiche or sour cream
- 2 Tbsp. prepared horseradish
- ¼ tsp. pepper
- 2 Tbsp. minced chives
  Hot cooked rice

In a large nonstick skillet, combine the beef tips with gravy, creme fraiche, horseradish and pepper. Cook and stir over medium-low heat until heated through. Sprinkle with chives and serve with rice.
⅔ cup: 365 cal., 28g fat (16g sat. fat), 98mg chol., 718mg sod., 7g carb. (3g sugars, 1g fiber), 19g pro.

WEEKDAY BEEF STEW

WEEKDAY BEEF STEW

Beef stew capped with flaky puff pastry adds comfort and joy to the weeknight menu. Make a salad and call folks to the table. They're going to love it!
—Daniel Anderson, Kenosha, WI

Takes: 30 min. • **Makes:** 4 servings

- 1 sheet frozen puff pastry, thawed
- 1 pkg. (15 oz.) refrigerated beef roast au jus
- 2 cans (14½ oz. each) diced tomatoes, undrained
- 1 pkg. (16 oz.) frozen vegetables for stew
- ¾ tsp. pepper
- 2 Tbsp. cornstarch
- 1¼ cups water

1. Preheat oven to 400°. Unfold puff pastry. Using a 4-in. round cookie cutter, cut out four circles. Place 2 in. apart on a greased baking sheet. Bake for 14-16 minutes or until golden brown.
2. Meanwhile, shred beef with two forks; transfer to a large saucepan. Add the tomatoes, vegetables and pepper; bring to a boil. In a small bowl, mix cornstarch and water until smooth; stir into the beef mixture. Return to a boil, stirring constantly; cook and stir 1-2 minutes or until thickened.
3. Ladle stew into four bowls; top each with a puff pastry round.
1½ cups with 1 pastry round: 604 cal., 25g fat (8g sat. fat), 73mg chol., 960mg sod., 65g carb. (10g sugars, 9g fiber), 32g pro.

JALAPENO POPPER QUESADILLAS

Quesadillas inspired by tasty poppers are a simple and fast solution when you're too busy to cook something complicated. If you like recipes with heat, this is for you.
—Rebecca Nisewonder, Richmond, IN

Takes: 25 min. • **Makes:** 4 servings

- 8 flour tortillas (8 in.)
- 1 carton (8 oz.) spreadable cream cheese
- ½ lb. bacon strips, cooked and crumbled
- 5 jalapeno peppers, seeded and finely chopped
- 2 cups shredded cheddar cheese

1. Preheat oven to 400°. Place half of the tortillas on two greased baking sheets. Spread with cream cheese; sprinkle with the bacon, jalapeno and cheese. Top with remaining tortillas.
2. Bake 8-10 minutes or until golden brown and cheese is melted.
1 quesadilla: 801 cal., 47g fat (23g sat. fat), 115mg chol., 1423mg sod., 60g carb. (3g sugars, 4g fiber), 33g pro.

★ ★ ★ ★ ★ **READER REVIEW**
"Absolutely delicious! Definitely will be making again! The bacon added great flavor with the spice of the jalapeno."
ANGEL182009 TASTEOFHOME.COM

CLASSIC BEEF WELLINGTONS

Perfect for special occasions, this entree is also impressively easy. You can find ready-made puff pastry sheets in the frozen food section.
—Kerry Dingwall, Wilmington, NC

Prep: 20 min. + chilling • **Bake:** 25 min.
Makes: 4 servings

- 4 beef tenderloin steaks (6 oz. each)
- ¾ tsp. salt, divided
- ½ tsp. pepper, divided
- 2 Tbsp. olive oil, divided
- 1¾ cups sliced fresh mushrooms
- 1 medium onion, chopped
- 1 pkg. (17.3 oz.) frozen puff pastry, thawed
- 1 large egg, lightly beaten

1. Sprinkle the steaks with ½ tsp. salt and ¼ tsp. pepper. In a large skillet, brown steaks in 1 Tbsp. oil for 2-3 minutes on each side. Remove from the skillet and refrigerate until chilled.

2. In the same skillet, saute mushrooms and onion in remaining oil until tender. Stir in remaining salt and pepper; cool to room temperature.
3. Preheat oven to 425°. On a lightly floured surface, roll each puff pastry sheet into a 14x9½-in. rectangle. Cut into two 7-in. squares (use scraps to make decorative cutouts if desired). Place a steak in the center of each square; top with mushroom mixture. Lightly brush pastry edges with water. Bring opposite corners of pastry over steak; pinch seams to seal tightly.
4. Place in a greased 15x10x1-in. baking pan. Cut four small slits in top of pastry. Arrange cutouts over top if desired. Brush with egg.
5. Bake 25-30 minutes or until pastry is golden brown and meat reaches desired doneness (for medium-rare, a thermometer should read 135°; medium, 140°; medium-well, 145°).
1 beef Wellington: 945 cal., 51g fat (13g sat. fat), 127mg chol., 866mg sod., 74g carb. (3g sugars, 10g fiber), 48g pro.

CLASSIC BEEF WELLINGTONS

HAMBURGER CASSEROLE

This casserole is such a hit it's traveled all over the country. My mother originated the recipe in Pennsylvania, I brought it to Texas when I married, I'm still making it in California, and my daughter treats her friends in Colorado to this oldie.
—Helen Carmichall, Santee, CA

Prep: 20 min. • **Cook:** 45 min.
Makes: 10 servings

2 lbs. lean ground beef (90% lean)
4 lbs. potatoes, peeled and sliced ¼ in. thick
1 large onion, sliced
1 tsp. salt
½ tsp. pepper
1 tsp. beef bouillon granules
1 cup boiling water
1 can (28 oz.) diced tomatoes, undrained
   Minced fresh parsley, optional

In a Dutch oven, layer half of the meat, potatoes and onion. Sprinkle with half of the salt and pepper. Repeat the layers. Dissolve bouillon in water; pour over all. Top with tomatoes. Cover and cook over medium heat for 45-50 minutes or until potatoes are tender. Garnish with parsley if desired.

1 cup: 270 cal., 8g fat (3g sat. fat), 57mg chol., 493mg sod., 30g carb. (5g sugars, 3g fiber), 21g pro. **Diabetic exchanges:** 3 lean meat, 2 starch.

BLUE CHEESE-CRUSTED SIRLOIN STEAKS

BLUE CHEESE-CRUSTED SIRLOIN STEAKS

According to my wife, this smothered steak is my specialty. I like to make it for her on Friday nights to help us wish the workweek farewell.
—Michael Rouse, Minot, ND

Takes: 30 min. • **Makes:** 4 servings

- 2 Tbsp. butter, divided
- 1 medium onion, chopped
- ⅓ cup crumbled blue cheese
- 2 Tbsp. soft bread crumbs
- 1 beef top sirloin steak (1 in. thick and 1½ lbs.)
- ¾ tsp. salt
- ½ tsp. pepper

1. Preheat broiler. In a large broil-safe skillet, heat 1 Tbsp. butter over medium heat; saute onion until tender. Transfer to a bowl; stir in cheese and bread crumbs.

2. Cut steak into four pieces; sprinkle with salt and pepper. In same pan, heat remaining butter over medium heat; cook steaks until desired doneness (for medium-rare, a thermometer should read 135°; medium, 140°), 4-5 minutes per side.

3. Spread onion mixture over steaks. Broil 4-6 in. from heat until lightly browned, 2-3 minutes.

Note: To make soft bread crumbs, tear bread into pieces and place in a food processor or blender. Cover and pulse until crumbs form. One slice of bread yields ½ to ¾ cup crumbs.

1 serving: 326 cal., 16g fat (8g sat. fat), 92mg chol., 726mg sod., 5g carb. (2g sugars, 1g fiber), 39g pro.

Balsamic Sirloin Steak Mix 3 Tbsp. balsamic vinegar and 3 tsp. steak sauce. Season steak with ½ tsp. pepper. Do not brown the steaks; broil as directed 5-7 minutes on each side or until desired doneness. Cut steak across the grain into ¼-in. slices. Place on a foil-lined baking sheet; drizzle with juices from cutting board and remaining steak sauce mixture. Top with 2 oz. Swiss cheese, cut into thin strips. Broil steak 1 minute or until cheese is melted.

Dressed-Up Sirloin Steak Mix 1 Tbsp. olive oil, 1½ tsp. minced garlic, 1 tsp. dried oregano and 1 tsp. pepper. Rub over both sides of steak. Brush with ¼ cup Catalina salad dressing. Do not brown steaks; broil steak as directed for 5-7 minutes on each side or until desired doneness. Serve with additional Catalina if desired.

TEST KITCHEN TIP
Not everyone is a fan of blue cheese, which has a strong flavor. If you want to try other aged cheeses, swap it out with Gorgonzola, Roquefort or aged goat cheese. For milder flavor try feta.

BACON-WRAPPED PESTO PORK TENDERLOIN

I love to serve this family-favorite pork tenderloin—maybe because of the compliments that come with it! When the weather warms up, we grill it instead.
—Megan Riofski, Frankfort, IL

Prep: 30 min. • **Bake:** 20 min.
Makes: 4 servings

- 10 **bacon strips**
- 1 **pork tenderloin (1 lb.)**
- ¼ **tsp. pepper**
- ⅓ **cup prepared pesto**
- 1 **cup shredded Italian cheese blend**
- 1 **cup fresh baby spinach**

1. Preheat oven to 425°. Arrange the bacon strips lengthwise in a foil-lined 15x10x1-in. pan, overlapping slightly.
2. Cut tenderloin lengthwise through the center to within ½ in. of bottom. Open tenderloin flat; cover with plastic wrap. Pound pork with a meat mallet to ½-in. thickness. Remove plastic; place the tenderloin on center of bacon strips, perpendicular to strips.
3. Sprinkle pepper over pork. Spread with pesto; layer the cheese and spinach. Close tenderloin; wrap with the bacon, overlapping ends. Tie tenderloin with kitchen string at 3-in. intervals. Secure the ends with toothpicks.
4. In a 12-in. skillet, brown roast on all sides, about 8 minutes. Return to baking pan; roast in oven until a thermometer inserted in pork reads 145°, 17-20 minutes. Remove string and toothpicks; let stand 5 minutes before slicing.

1 serving: 402 cal., 25g fat (9g sat. fat), 104mg chol., 864mg sod., 4g carb. (1g sugars, 1g fiber), 37g pro.

BACON-WRAPPED PESTO PORK TENDERLOIN

**ROSEMARY
TURKEY BREAST
PG 73**

Poultry & Seafood

For flavor and convenience, you can't go wrong with these succulent main courses. Chicken, turkey, fish and shrimp make even the easiest dinners feel special.

CAESAR SALMON WITH ROASTED TOMATOES & ARTICHOKES

CAESAR SALMON WITH ROASTED TOMATOES & ARTICHOKES

Everyone needs a go-to recipe for quick dinners, and this is mine. Treat family or weekend guests like royalty when you serve salmon and vegetables elegantly prepared with a little Caesar.
—Mary Hawkes, Prescott, AZ

Takes: 25 min. • **Makes:** 4 servings

- 4 salmon fillets (5 oz. each)
- 5 Tbsp. reduced-fat Caesar vinaigrette, divided
- ¼ tsp. pepper, divided
- 2 cups grape tomatoes
- 1 can (14 oz.) water-packed artichoke hearts, drained and quartered
- 1 medium sweet orange or yellow pepper, cut into 1-in. pieces

1. Preheat oven to 425°. Place salmon fillets on one half of a 15x10x1-in. baking pan coated with cooking spray. Brush the salmon with 2 Tbsp. vinaigrette; sprinkle with ⅛ tsp. pepper.
2. In a large bowl, combine the tomatoes, artichoke hearts and sweet pepper. Add remaining vinaigrette and pepper; toss to coat. Place tomato mixture on remaining half of pan. Roast 12-15 minutes or until fish just begins to flake easily with a fork and the vegetables are tender.

1 fillet with ¾ cup tomato mixture: 318 cal., 16g fat (3g sat. fat), 73mg chol., 674mg sod., 12g carb. (4g sugars, 2g fiber), 28g pro. **Diabetic exchanges:** 4 lean meat, 1 vegetable, 1 fat.

CHICKEN PROVOLONE

CHICKEN PROVOLONE

This chicken entree is one of my simplest dishes—and one of my husband's favorites. The fresh basil really comes through in every bite.
—Dawn E. Bryant, Thedford, NE

Takes: 25 min.
Makes: 4 servings

- 4 boneless skinless chicken breast halves (4 oz. each)
- ¼ tsp. pepper
  Butter-flavored cooking spray
- 8 fresh basil leaves
- 4 thin slices prosciutto or deli ham
- 4 slices provolone cheese

1. Sprinkle chicken with pepper. In a large nonstick skillet coated with butter-flavored cooking spray, cook the chicken over medium heat for 4-5 minutes on each side or until a thermometer reads 170°.
2. Transfer to an ungreased baking sheet; top with basil, prosciutto and cheese. Broil 6-8 in. from the heat for 1-2 minutes or until cheese is melted.

1 serving: 236 cal., 11g fat (6g sat. fat), 89mg chol., 435mg sod., 1g carb. (0 sugars, 0 fiber), 33g pro. **Diabetic exchanges:** 4 lean meat.

MEDITERRANEAN CHICKEN

CONTEST-WINNING BROCCOLI CHICKEN CASSEROLE

This delicious twist on chicken divan came from an old boss, who gave the recipe to me when I got married. It's fast, satisfying comfort food.
—Jennifer Schlachter, Big Rock, IL

Prep: 15 min. • **Bake:** 30 min.
Makes: 6 servings

- 1 pkg. (6 oz.) chicken stuffing mix
- 2 cups cubed cooked chicken
- 1 cup frozen broccoli florets, thawed
- 1 can (10¾ oz.) condensed broccoli cheese soup, undiluted
- 1 cup shredded cheddar cheese

1. Preheat oven to 350°. Prepare stuffing mix according to the package directions, using 1½ cups water.
2. In large bowl, combine the chicken, broccoli and soup; transfer to a greased 11x7-in. baking dish. Top with stuffing; sprinkle with cheese. Bake, covered, for 20 minutes. Uncover; bake 10-15 minutes longer or until heated through.
Freeze option: Place individual portions of cooled casserole in freezer containers; freeze. To use, partially thaw overnight in refrigerator. Transfer to a microwave-safe dish; microwave, covered, on high until a thermometer inserted in the center reads 165°, stirring occasionally and adding a little broth if necessary.
1⅓ cups: 315 cal., 13g fat (6g sat. fat), 66mg chol., 1025mg sod., 25g carb. (4g sugars, 2g fiber), 23g pro.

TEST KITCHEN TIP
Punch up the flavor a bit with rosemary, thyme or any of your favorite herbs or seasonings. Add a pinch to the chicken-broccoli mixture before transferring into the baking pan.

MEDITERRANEAN CHICKEN

Chicken goes Mediterranean in this skillet creation, a warm welcome to the table.
—Mary Relyea, Canastota, NY

Takes: 25 min. • **Makes:** 4 servings

- 4 boneless skinless chicken breast halves (6 oz. each)
- ¼ tsp. salt
- ¼ tsp. pepper
- 3 Tbsp. olive oil
- 1 pint grape tomatoes
- 16 pitted Greek or ripe olives, sliced
- 3 Tbsp. capers, drained

1. Preheat oven to 475°. Sprinkle chicken with salt and pepper. In a large ovenproof skillet, cook chicken in oil over medium heat for 2-3 minutes on each side or until golden brown. Add the tomatoes, olives and capers.
2. Bake, uncovered, for 10-14 minutes or until a thermometer reads 170°.
1 serving: 336 cal., 18g fat (3g sat. fat), 94mg chol., 631mg sod., 6g carb. (3g sugars, 2g fiber), 36g pro.

BREADED BAKED TILAPIA

So much flavor from so few ingredients! An easy crumb coating makes this yummy tilapia ideal for busy weeknights. Try the breading on cod for a change of pace.
—Brandi Castillo, Santa Maria, CA

Takes: 20 min. **Makes:** 4 servings

- ¾ cup soft bread crumbs
- ⅓ cup grated Parmesan cheese
- 1 tsp. garlic salt
- 1 tsp. dried oregano
- 4 tilapia fillets (5 oz. each)

1. Preheat oven to 425°. In a shallow bowl, combine bread crumbs, cheese, garlic salt and oregano. Coat fillets in crumb mixture. Place on a baking sheet coated with cooking spray.
2. Bake 8-12 minutes or until fish flakes easily with a fork.
1 fillet: 143 cal., 2g fat (1g sat. fat), 72mg chol., 356mg sod., 2g carb. (0 sugars, 0 fiber), 28g pro. **Diabetic exchanges:** 4 lean meat.

MANGO CHUTNEY CHICKEN CURRY

My father dreamed up this tasty curry and chutney combination. Now my family cooks it on road trips—in rain and sun, in the mountains, even on the beach. Adjust the curry for taste and heat.
—Dina Moreno, Seattle, WA

Takes: 25 min. • **Makes:** 4 servings

- 1 Tbsp. canola oil
- 1 lb. boneless skinless chicken breasts, cubed
- 1 Tbsp. curry powder
- 2 garlic cloves, minced
- ¼ tsp. salt
- ¼ tsp. pepper
- ½ cup mango chutney
- ½ cup half-and-half cream

1. In a large skillet, heat oil over medium-high heat; brown chicken. Stir in curry powder, garlic, salt and pepper; cook 1-2 minutes longer or until aromatic.
2. Stir in chutney and cream. Bring to boil. Reduce heat; simmer, uncovered, 4-6 minutes or until chicken is no longer pink, stirring occasionally.
½ cup: 320 cal., 9g fat (3g sat. fat), 78mg chol., 558mg sod., 30g carb. (19g sugars, 1g fiber), 24g pro.

PECAN-COCONUT CRUSTED TILAPIA

When I entertain guests with dietary restrictions, tilapia coated in pecans and coconut makes everyone happy. It's gluten-free and loaded with flavor.
—Caitlin Roth, Chicago, IL

Takes: 25 min. • **Makes:** 4 servings

- 2 large eggs
- ½ cup unsweetened finely shredded coconut
- ½ cup finely chopped pecans
- ½ tsp. salt
- ¼ tsp. crushed red pepper flakes
- 4 tilapia fillets (6 oz. each)
- 2 Tbsp. canola oil

1. In a shallow bowl, whisk the eggs. In a separate shallow bowl, combine coconut, pecans, salt and pepper flakes. Dip fillets in eggs, then in coconut mixture, patting to help coating adhere.
2. In a large skillet, heat oil over medium heat. In batches, add the tilapia and cook 2-3 minutes on each side or until fish is lightly browned and begins to flake easily with a fork.
Note: Look for unsweetened coconut in the baking or health food section.
1 fillet: 380 cal., 26g fat (8g sat. fat), 129mg chol., 377mg sod., 4g carb. (1g sugars, 3g fiber), 35g pro.
Parmesan-Crusted Tilapia Omit coconut, pecans and pepper flakes. In a shallow bowl, combine ½ cup crushed Ritz crackers, ¼ cup grated Parmesan cheese and salt. Proceed as directed.

MANGO CHUTNEY CHICKEN CURRY

CHICKEN & WAFFLES

CHICKEN & WAFFLES

My first experience with chicken and waffles sent my taste buds into orbit. I first made this dish as an appetizer, but we all love it as a main course, too.
—Lisa Renshaw, Kansas City, MO

Takes: 25 min.
Makes: 4 servings

- 12 frozen crispy chicken strips (about 18 oz.)
- ½ cup honey
- 2 tsp. hot pepper sauce
- 8 frozen waffles, toasted

1. Bake chicken strips according to package directions. Meanwhile, in a small bowl, mix the honey and pepper sauce.
2. Cut chicken into bite-size pieces; serve on waffles. Drizzle with honey mixture.
1 serving: 643 cal., 22g fat (3g sat. fat), 32mg chol., 958mg sod., 93g carb. (39g sugars, 6g fiber), 21g pro.

TURKEY TENDERLOINS WITH SHALLOT BERRY SAUCE

The original recipe called for chicken and apricot, but I decided to try turkey and berry jam to use up some leftovers. I was thrilled with how very well it turned out.
—Kendra Doss, Colorado Springs, CO

Prep: 15 min.
Cook: 25 min.
Makes: 8 servings

- 4 turkey breast tenderloins (12 oz. each)
- ½ tsp. salt
- ½ tsp. pepper
- 1 Tbsp. olive oil
- ¼ cup chicken broth

SAUCE
- 1 Tbsp. olive oil
- 5 shallots, thinly sliced
- ¼ tsp. salt
- ¼ tsp. pepper
- ½ cup chicken broth
- ¼ cup balsamic vinegar
- 3 Tbsp. seedless raspberry jam

1. Sprinkle turkey with salt and pepper. In a large skillet, heat oil over medium heat; brown the tenderloins in batches. Cook, covered, 8-10 minutes longer or until a thermometer reads 165°. Remove from pan; keep warm.
2. Add broth to skillet; increase heat to medium-high. Cook, stirring to loosen browned bits from pan; remove from the heat.
3. Meanwhile, in another skillet, heat oil over medium-high heat. Add shallots, salt and pepper; cook and stir until shallots are tender. Add broth, stirring to loosen the browned bits from pan. Stir in vinegar and jam. Bring sauce to a boil; cook until mixture is slightly thickened, 4-5 minutes, stirring occasionally.
4. Slice tenderloins; drizzle with the pan juices. Serve with berry sauce.
1 serving: 258 cal., 6g fat (0 sat. fat), 68mg chol., 414mg sod., 12g carb. (8g sugars, 0 fiber), 43g pro. **Diabetic exchanges:** 5 lean meat, 1 starch, ½ fat.

GINGER-CHUTNEY SHRIMP STIR-FRY

I made this recipe a lot when I was juggling college, work and a growing family. The ginger and chutney produce big flavor in hardly any time.
—Sally Sibthorpe, Shelby Township, MI

Takes: 25 min. • **Makes:** 4 servings

- 2 Tbsp. peanut or canola oil
- 1 lb. uncooked medium shrimp, peeled and deveined, tails removed
- 1 Tbsp. minced fresh gingerroot
- 3 cups frozen pepper and onion stir-fry blend, thawed
- ¾ cup mango chutney
- 2 Tbsp. water
- ¾ tsp. salt
   Hot cooked rice, optional

In a large skillet, heat oil over medium-high heat. Add shrimp and ginger; stir-fry for 4-5 minutes or until shrimp turn pink. Stir in remaining ingredients; cook until the vegetables are crisp-tender, stirring occasionally. If desired, serve with rice.

1 cup: 356 cal., 8g fat (1g sat. fat), 138mg chol., 1102mg sod., 47g carb. (30g sugars, 1g fiber), 19g pro.

★ ★ ★ ★ ★ **READER REVIEW**

"Marvelous ! I make a lot of dishes with shrimp, but I would never have thought to add mango to the mix. I will definitely make this again."

BEEMA TASTEOFHOME.COM

GINGER-CHUTNEY SHRIMP STIR-FRY

SHRIMP & FETA SKILLET

SHRIMP & FETA SKILLET

My friend's feisty Italian grandmother, Gemma, makes a dish similar to my shrimp with tomatoes. When I make it, I think of Gemma and smile.
—Celeste Ehrenberg, Topeka, KS

Takes: 25 min. • **Makes:** 4 servings

- 2 cans (14½ oz. each) diced tomatoes with basil, oregano and garlic, undrained
- 2 tsp. garlic powder
- 2 tsp. dried basil
- 1¼ lbs. uncooked shrimp (31-40 per lb.), peeled and deveined
- 1 cup crumbled feta cheese
  Crusty whole grain bread, optional

1. In a large skillet, combine tomatoes, garlic powder and basil; bring to a boil. Reduce heat; simmer, uncovered, for 4-6 minutes or until slightly thickened.
2. Add shrimp; cook and stir 3-4 minutes or until shrimp turn pink. Sprinkle feta over shrimp; serve with bread if desired.

1¼ cups: 261 cal., 6g fat (3g sat. fat), 187mg chol., 1092mg sod., 15g carb. (7g sugars, 5g fiber), 30g pro.

RASPBERRY CHICKEN

Basic skillet-cooked chicken gets a slightly sweet kick with this fresh, fun raspberry sauce, and it's scrumptious over rice.
—Anita Hennesy, Hagerstown, MD

Takes: 30 min. • **Makes:** 4 servings

- 4 boneless skinless chicken breast halves (5 oz. each)
- ¼ tsp. salt
- ¼ tsp. pepper
- ½ cup seedless raspberry jam
- 2 Tbsp. balsamic vinegar
- 1 Tbsp. reduced-sodium soy sauce
- ⅛ tsp. crushed red pepper flakes

1. Sprinkle chicken with salt and pepper. In a large nonstick skillet coated with cooking spray, cook the chicken over medium heat 5-7 minutes on each side or until a thermometer reads 170°.
2. Meanwhile, in a small saucepan, mix the remaining ingredients. Bring sauce to a boil; cook until liquid is reduced to ½ cup. Serve with chicken.

1 serving: 260 cal., 3g fat (1g sat. fat), 78mg chol., 369mg sod., 28g carb. (25g sugars, 0 fiber), 29g pro. **Diabetic exchanges:** 4 lean meat, 1½ starch.

ROSEMARY TURKEY BREAST

I season turkey with a blend of rosemary, garlic and paprika. Because I rub the blend directly on the meat under the skin, I can remove the skin before serving and not lose any of the flavor. Lower-in-fat with remarkable flavor, this is an entree that serves as a centerpiece for special meals.
—Dorothy Pritchett, Wills Point, TX

Prep: 10 min. • **Bake:** 1½ hours + standing
Makes: 15 servings

- 2 Tbsp. olive oil
- 8 to 10 garlic cloves, peeled
- 3 Tbsp. chopped fresh rosemary or 3 tsp. dried rosemary, crushed
- 1 tsp. salt
- 1 tsp. paprika
- ½ tsp. coarsely ground pepper
- 1 bone-in turkey breast (5 lbs.)

1. Preheat oven to 325°. In the bowl of a food processor, combine oil, garlic and seasonings; cover and process until garlic is coarsely chopped.
2. With your fingers, carefully loosen the skin from both sides of turkey breast. Spread half of the garlic mixture over the meat under the skin. Smooth skin over meat and secure to underside of breast with toothpicks. Spread remaining garlic mixture over turkey skin.
3. Place the turkey breast on a rack in a shallow roasting pan. Bake, uncovered, for 1½-2 hours or until a thermometer reads 170°. Let stand for 15 minutes before slicing. Discard the toothpicks.
4 oz. cooked turkey: 148 cal., 3g fat (0 sat. fat), 78mg chol., 207mg sod., 1g carb. (0 sugars, 0 fiber), 29g pro. **Diabetic exchanges:** 4 lean meat.

ROSEMARY TURKEY BREAST

PESTO GRILLED SALMON

Buttery, colorful and flaky, this rich and impressive salmon will be a family favorite in moments. Five smart ingredients give you the perfect meal for a large dinner party.
—Sonya Labbe, West Hollywood, CA

Takes: 30 min. • **Makes:** 12 servings

- 1 salmon fillet (3 lbs.)
- ½ cup prepared pesto
- 2 green onions, finely chopped
- ¼ cup lemon juice
- 2 garlic cloves, minced

1. Moisten a paper towel with cooking oil; using long-handled tongs, lightly coat the grill rack. Place the salmon skin side down on grill rack. Grill, covered, over medium heat or broil 4 in. from the heat about 5 minutes.
2. In a small bowl, combine the pesto, onions, lemon juice and garlic. Carefully spoon some of the pesto mixture over salmon. Grill 15-20 minutes longer or until the fish flakes easily with a fork, basting occasionally with the remaining pesto mixture.
3 oz. cooked salmon: 262 cal., 17g fat (4g sat. fat), 70mg chol., 147mg sod., 1g carb. (0 sugars, 0 fiber), 25g pro.
Diabetic exchanges: 3 lean meat, 3 fat.
Glazed Asian Salmon Replace basting ingredients with a mixture of ½ cup soy sauce, ¼ cup brown sugar, ½ tsp. each crushed red pepper flakes and ground ginger, and ¼ tsp. sesame oil. Grill and baste salmon as directed.
Herbed Salmon Place salmon on double thickness of heavy-duty foil. Mix ½ cup softened butter with ¼ cup each minced fresh chives, tarragon and thyme; spread over salmon. Top with ⅓ cup finely chopped red onion, ¼ tsp. each salt and pepper, and 1 thinly sliced lemon. Seal foil and grill 20-25 minutes. Open carefully to allow steam to escape.

SLOW COOKER TURKEY BREAST

Try this wonderfully flavored, easy-to-make, tender slow cooker entree when you're craving turkey.
—Maria Juco, Milwaukee, WI

Prep: 10 min. • **Cook:** 5 hours
Makes: 14 servings

- 1   bone-in turkey breast (6 to 7 lbs.), skin removed
- 1   Tbsp. olive oil
- 1   tsp. dried minced garlic
- 1   tsp. seasoned salt
- 1   tsp. paprika
- 1   tsp. Italian seasoning
- 1   tsp. pepper
- ½   cup water

Brush turkey with oil. Combine the garlic, seasoned salt, paprika, Italian seasoning and pepper; rub over turkey. Transfer to a 6-qt. slow cooker; add water. Cover and cook on low for 5-6 hours or until tender.
4 oz. cooked turkey: 174 cal., 2g fat (0 sat. fat), 101mg chol., 172mg sod., 0 carb. (0 sugars, 0 fiber), 37g pro. **Diabetic exchanges:** 4 lean meat.
Lemon-Garlic Turkey Breast Combine ¼ cup minced fresh parsley, 8 minced garlic cloves, 4 tsp. grated lemon peel, 2 tsp. salt-free lemon-pepper seasoning and 1½ tsp. salt; rub over turkey breast. Add water and cook as directed.

TEST KITCHEN TIP

Out of Italian seasoning? Blend your own by by substituting ¼ teaspoon each of basil, thyme, rosemary and oregano for each teaspoon of Italian seasoning called for in a recipe.

MEXICAN RICE WITH CHICKEN

This skillet supper comes together with leftover cooked chicken and a packaged mix. The next day, I'll serve any leftovers on tortillas with cheese and sour cream. Both meals are a hit.
—Debra Rzodkiewicz, Erie, PA

Prep: 5 min. • **Cook:** 30 min.
Makes: 4 servings

- 1   pkg. (6.4 oz.) Mexican-style rice and pasta mix
- 2   Tbsp. butter
- 1¾ cups water
- 1   can (14½ oz.) diced tomatoes with onions, undrained
- 2   cups cubed cooked chicken
- 1   jalapeno pepper, seeded and chopped

1. In a large skillet, cook and stir rice and pasta mix in butter until lightly browned, about 5 minutes. Add water, tomatoes and contents of rice seasoning packet. Bring to a boil. Reduce heat; cover and cook for 10 minutes.
2. Add the chicken and jalapeno. Cover and cook for 8-10 minutes or until rice is tender and liquid is absorbed.
Note: This recipe was tested using Rice-A-Roni rice and pasta mix. When cutting hot peppers, disposable gloves are recommended. Avoid touching face.
1½ cups: 385 cal., 12g fat (5g sat. fat), 79mg chol., 1217mg sod., 42g carb. (9g sugars, 2g fiber), 25g pro.

MEXICAN RICE WITH CHICKEN

SCALLOPS WITH WILTED SPINACH

ZESTY CHICKEN SOFT TACOS

We've made these tacos with corn and flour tortillas, but naan flatbread is our favorite. Set out toppings and let people make their own.
—Jessie Grearson-Sapat, Falmouth, ME

Takes: 25 min. • **Makes:** 6 servings

- 1 cup reduced-fat sour cream
- 2 Tbsp. Sriracha Asian hot chili sauce
- 2 Tbsp. lime juice
- 1½ tsp. grated lime zest
- ½ tsp. salt
- ⅛ tsp. pepper
- 6 naan flatbreads, warmed
- 1 rotisserie chicken, skin removed, shredded
  Minced fresh cilantro, optional

In a bowl, mix the first six ingredients. Spread over flatbreads; top with chicken and, if desired, cilantro.

1 taco: 420 cal., 14g fat (5g sat. fat), 111mg chol., 942mg sod., 33g carb. (7g sugars, 1g fiber), 37g pro.

SCALLOPS WITH WILTED SPINACH

Two of my favorite foods are bacon and seafood. This dish brings them together with white wine, shallots and fresh baby spinach. Serve with bread to soak up the tasty broth.
—Deborah Williams, Peoria, AZ

Takes: 25 min.
Makes: 4 servings

- 4 bacon strips, chopped
- 12 sea scallops (about 1½ lbs.), side muscles removed
- 2 shallots, finely chopped
- ½ cup white wine or chicken broth
- 8 cups fresh baby spinach (about 8 oz.)

1. In a large nonstick skillet, cook bacon over medium heat until crisp, stirring occasionally. Remove with a slotted spoon; drain on paper towels. Discard drippings, reserving 2 Tbsp. Wipe skillet clean if necessary.
2. Pat scallops dry with paper towels. In same skillet, heat 1 Tbsp. drippings over medium-high heat. Add scallops; cook 2-3 minutes on each side or until golden brown and firm. Remove from the pan; keep warm.
3. Heat remaining drippings in same pan over medium-high heat. Add shallots; cook and stir 2-3 minutes or until tender. Add the wine; bring to a boil, stirring to loosen browned bits from pan. Add the spinach; cook and stir for 1-2 minutes or until wilted. Stir in bacon. Serve spinach with the scallops.

3 scallops with ½ cup spinach mixture: 247 cal., 11g fat (4g sat. fat), 56mg chol., 964mg sod., 12g carb. (1g sugars, 1g fiber), 26g pro.

SHRIMP FRIED RICE

QUICK CHICKEN PICCATA

Laced with lemon and simmered in white wine, here's a stovetop entree that is both easy and elegant. Most any side—noodles or veggies or bread—tastes better next to this lovely chicken.
—Cynthia Heil, Augusta, GA

Takes: 30 min. • **Makes:** 4 servings

- ¼ cup all-purpose flour
- ½ tsp. salt
- ½ tsp. pepper
- 4 boneless skinless chicken breast halves (4 oz. each)
- ¼ cup butter, cubed
- ¼ cup white wine or chicken broth
- 1 Tbsp. lemon juice
  Minced fresh parsley, optional

1. In a shallow bowl, mix flour, salt and pepper. Pound chicken breasts with a meat mallet to ½-in. thickness. Dip chicken in flour mixture to coat both sides; shake off excess.
2. In a large skillet, heat the butter over medium heat. Brown chicken on both sides. Add wine; bring to a boil. Reduce heat; simmer, uncovered, 12-15 minutes or until chicken is no longer pink. Drizzle with the lemon juice. If desired, sprinkle with parsley.
1 chicken breast half with about 1 Tbsp. sauce: 265 cal., 14g fat (8g sat. fat), 93mg chol., 442mg sod., 7g carb. (0 sugars, 0 fiber), 24g pro.

SHRIMP FRIED RICE

This delectable shrimp dish is filled with color and flavor, and our family of four can't get enough of it. Crumbled bacon adds crispness and heartiness. Consider this stir-fry when you crave a new entree.
—Sandra Thompson, White Hall, AR

Takes: 20 min.
Makes: 8 servings

- 4 Tbsp. butter, divided
- 4 large eggs, lightly beaten
- 3 cups cold cooked rice
- 1 pkg. (16 oz.) frozen mixed vegetables
- 1 lb. uncooked medium shrimp, peeled and deveined
- ½ tsp. salt
- ¼ tsp. pepper
- 8 bacon strips, cooked and crumbled, optional

1. In a large skillet, melt 1 Tbsp. butter over medium-high heat. Pour the eggs into skillet. As eggs set, lift edges, letting the uncooked portion flow underneath. Remove eggs and keep warm.
2. Melt remaining butter in skillet. Add rice, vegetables and shrimp; cook and stir for 5 minutes or until shrimp turn pink. Meanwhile, chop eggs into small pieces. Return eggs to the pan; sprinkle with salt and pepper. Cook until heated through, stirring occasionally. Sprinkle with bacon if desired.
1 cup: 241 cal., 9g fat (4g sat. fat), 206mg chol., 354mg sod., 24g carb. (2g sugars, 3g fiber), 15g pro.

Family Classic

QUICK CHICKEN PICCATA

CHICKEN ENCHILADA BAKE

CHICKEN ENCHILADA BAKE

This recipe makes a lot, which is a good thing, because people will be saying, "More, please." Green enchilada sauce brightens up this southwestern casserole.
—Melanie Burns, Pueblo West, CO

Prep: 20 min. • **Bake:** 50 min. + standing
Makes: 10 servings

- 4½ cups shredded rotisserie chicken
- 1 can (28 oz.) green enchilada sauce
- 1¼ cups sour cream
- 9 corn tortillas (6 in.), cut into 1½-in. pieces
- 4 cups shredded Monterey Jack cheese

1. Preheat oven to 375°. In a greased 13x9-in. baking dish, layer half of the chicken, enchilada sauce, sour cream, tortillas and cheese. Repeat layers.
2. Bake, covered, 40 minutes. Uncover; bake until bubbly, about 10 minutes. Let stand 15 minutes before serving.
Freeze option: Cover and freeze the unbaked casserole. To use, partially thaw in refrigerator overnight. Remove from refrigerator 30 minutes before baking. Preheat oven to 375°. Bake casserole as directed, increasing time as necessary to heat through and for a thermometer inserted in center to read 165°.
1 cup: 469 cal., 29g fat (14g sat. fat), 113mg chol., 1077mg sod., 16g carb. (3g sugars, 1g fiber), 34g pro.

TEST KITCHEN TIP
For extra flair and flavor, add layers of frozen corn kernels or canned black beans that you've rinsed and drained.

COD WITH BACON & BALSAMIC TOMATOES

PECAN-CRUSTED CATFISH

Mustard and dill give this catfish its savory flavor, and the pecan crust lends a delightful crunch.
—*Taste of Home* Test Kitchen

Takes: 20 min. • **Makes:** 2 servings

- 2 Tbsp. Dijon mustard
- 1 Tbsp. 2% milk
- ¼ tsp. dill weed
- ½ cup ground pecans
- 2 catfish fillets (6 oz. each)

1. Preheat oven to 425°. In a shallow bowl, combine mustard, milk and dill. Place pecans in another shallow bowl. Dip fillets in the mustard mixture and then in pecans. Place on a baking sheet coated with cooking spray.
2. Bake for 10-12 minutes or until fish flakes easily with a fork.

1 serving: 341 cal., 23g fat (4g sat. fat), 80mg chol., 333mg sod., 4g carb. (1g sugars, 1g fiber), 29g pro.

COD WITH BACON & BALSAMIC TOMATOES

Let's face it, everything really is better with bacon. I fry it up, add cod fillets to the pan and finish with a big, tomato-y pop that's both pretty and light.
—Maureen McClanahan, St. Louis, MO

Takes: 30 min. • **Makes:** 4 servings

- 4 center-cut bacon strips, chopped
- 4 cod fillets (5 oz. each)
- ½ tsp. salt
- ¼ tsp. pepper
- 2 cups grape tomatoes, halved
- 2 Tbsp. balsamic vinegar

1. In a large skillet, cook chopped bacon over medium heat until crisp, stirring occasionally. Remove the pieces with a slotted spoon; drain on paper towels.
2. Sprinkle the fillets with salt and pepper. Add fillets to bacon drippings; cook over medium-high heat 4-6 minutes on each side or until fish just begins to flake easily with a fork. Remove and keep warm.
3. Add the tomatoes to skillet; cook and stir for 2-4 minutes or until softened. Stir in vinegar; reduce heat to medium-low. Cook 1-2 minutes longer or until sauce is thickened. Serve the cod with tomato mixture and bacon.

1 fillet with ¼ cup tomato mixture and 1 Tbsp. bacon: 178 cal., 6g fat (2g sat. fat), 64mg chol., 485mg sod., 5g carb. (4g sugars, 1g fiber), 26g pro. **Diabetic exchanges:** 4 lean meat, 1 vegetable.

PARMESAN-RANCH
PAN ROLLS
PG 89

Sides & Breads

Don't make side dishes an afterthought. These quick, easy sides and breads won't get lost in the shuffle—and they might just steal the show!

MINTY SUGAR SNAP PEAS

MINTY SUGAR SNAP PEAS
Fresh mint is great touch on cooked sugar snap peas. It's also nice on green beans or carrots.
—Alice Kaldahl, Ray, ND

Takes: 10 min. • **Makes:** 4 servings

- 3 cups fresh sugar snap peas, trimmed
- ¼ tsp. sugar
- 2 to 3 Tbsp. minced fresh mint
- 2 Tbsp. butter

Place 1 in. of water in a large skillet. Add peas and sugar; bring to a boil. Reduce heat; simmer, covered, until peas are crisp-tender, 4-5 minutes; drain. Stir in mint and butter.

¾ cup: 102 cal., 6g fat (4g sat. fat), 15mg chol., 45mg sod., 9g carb. (4g sugars, 3g fiber), 4g pro. **Diabetic exchanges:** 2 vegetable, 1½ fat.

MUSHROOM & PEAS RICE PILAF
Anything goes in a rice pilaf, so I add peas and baby portobello mushrooms for extra color, texture and a touch of style.
—Stacy Mullens, Gresham, OR

Takes: 25 min. • **Makes:** 6 servings

- 1 pkg. (6.6 oz.) rice pilaf mix with toasted almonds
- 1 Tbsp. butter
- 1½ cups fresh or frozen peas
- 1 cup sliced baby portobello mushrooms

1. Prepare pilaf according to package directions.
2. In a large skillet, heat the butter over medium heat. Add peas and mushrooms; cook and stir until tender, 6-8 minutes. Stir in rice.

⅔ cup: 177 cal., 6g fat (2g sat. fat), 10mg chol., 352mg sod., 28g carb. (3g sugars, 3g fiber), 5g pro. **Diabetic exchanges:** 2 starch, ½ fat.

OAT DINNER ROLLS

These rolls are out of this world. The addition of oats makes them a little heartier than most soft dinner rolls.
—Patricia Rutherford, Winchester, IL

Prep: 30 min. + rising • **Bake:** 20 min.
Makes: 2 dozen

2⅓ cups water, divided
1 cup quick-cooking oats
⅔ cup packed brown sugar
3 Tbsp. butter
1½ tsp. salt
2 pkg. (¼ oz. each) active dry yeast
5 to 5¾ cups all-purpose flour

1. In a large saucepan, bring 2 cups of water to a boil. Stir in oats; reduce heat. Simmer, uncovered, for 1 minute. Stir in brown sugar, butter, salt and the remaining water.
2. Transfer to a large bowl; let stand until mixture reaches 110°-115°. Stir in yeast. Add 3 cups flour; beat well. Add enough remaining flour to form a soft dough.
3. Turn dough onto a floured surface; knead until smooth and elastic, about 6-8 minutes. Place in a greased bowl; turn once to grease top. Cover and let rise in a warm place until doubled, about 1 hour.
4. Punch dough down; shape into 24 rolls. Place on greased baking sheets. Cover and let rise until doubled, about 30 minutes. Preheat oven to 350°.
5. Bake for 20-25 minutes or until golden brown. Remove from pan and cool on wire racks.

1 roll: 132 cal., 1g fat (0 sat. fat), 0 chol., 150mg sod., 28g carb. (6g sugars, 1g fiber), 3g pro.

OAT DINNER ROLLS

PULL-APART
BACON BREAD

Family
Classic

PULL-APART BACON BREAD

I stumbled across this recipe while I was looking for something different to take to a brunch. Boy, am I glad I did! It's a perfect treat to bake for an informal get-together. Everyone who asked for the recipe was surprised it called for just five ingredients.
—Traci Collins, Cheyenne, WY

Prep: 20 min. + rising • **Bake:** 55 min.
Makes: 16 servings (1 loaf)

- 12 bacon strips, diced
- 1 loaf (1 lb.) frozen bread dough, thawed
- 2 Tbsp. olive oil, divided
- 1 cup shredded part-skim mozzarella cheese
- 1 envelope (1 oz.) ranch salad dressing mix

1. In a large skillet, cook the bacon over medium heat for 5 minutes or until partially cooked; drain on paper towels. Roll out dough to ½-in. thickness; brush with 1 Tbsp. of oil. Cut into 1-in. pieces; place in a large bowl. Add the bacon, cheese, dressing mix and the remaining oil; toss to coat.

2. Arrange pieces in a 9x5-in. oval on a parchment paper-lined baking sheet, layering as needed. Cover and let rise in a warm place for 30 minutes or until doubled in size. Preheat oven to 350°.

3. Bake for 40 minutes. Cover with foil; bake 15 minutes longer or until loaf is golden brown.

1 serving: 149 cal., 6g fat (2g sat. fat), 8mg chol., 621mg sod., 17g carb. (1g sugars, 1g fiber), 6g pro.

WHITE BEANS & SPINACH

WHITE BEANS & SPINACH

This skillet side dish is a variation of a recipe I received from my Italian mother. I've prepared spinach this way for many years—especially since my children love it this way!
—Lucia Johnson, Massena, NY

Takes: 10 min. • **Makes:** 2 servings

- 2 Tbsp. water
- 2 garlic cloves, minced
- 8 cups fresh spinach (about 6 oz.)
- ¾ cup canned cannellini or white kidney beans, rinsed and drained
- ⅛ tsp. salt
  Dash cayenne pepper
  Dash ground nutmeg

Place water, garlic and spinach in a large skillet. Cook, covered, over medium heat just until tender, about 2-3 minutes, stirring occasionally. Stir in the remaining ingredients; heat through.

½ cup: 116 cal., 1g fat (0 sat. fat), 0 chol., 561mg sod., 21g carb. (1g sugars, 7g fiber), 7g pro. **Diabetic exchanges:** 1½ starch.

HERBED BUTTERNUT SQUASH

Butternut squash is a winter staple in our house. This is one of the many ways we prepare it—and one of our favorites.
—Jenn Tidwell, Fair Oaks, CA

Takes: 25 min. • **Makes:** 6 servings

- 1 medium butternut squash (about 3 lbs.)
- 1 Tbsp. olive oil
- 1½ tsp. dried oregano
- 1 tsp. dried thyme
- ½ tsp. salt
- ¼ tsp. pepper

Peel and cut the squash crosswise into ½-in.-thick slices; remove and discard seeds. In a large bowl, toss squash with the remaining ingredients. Grill, covered, over medium heat or broil 4 in. from heat 6-8 minutes on each side or until tender.

1 serving: 108 cal., 2g fat (0 sat. fat), 0 chol., 205mg sod., 23g carb. (5g sugars, 7g fiber), 2g pro. **Diabetic exchanges:** 1½ starch, ½ fat.

CHEDDAR CORN DOG MUFFINS

I wanted a change from hot dogs, so I made corn dog muffins. I added jalapenos to this kid-friendly recipe and that won my husband over, too.
—Becky Tarala, Palm Coast, FL

Takes: 25 min. • **Makes:** 9 muffins

- 1 pkg. (8½ oz.) corn bread/muffin mix
- ⅔ cup 2% milk
- 1 large egg, lightly beaten
- 5 turkey hot dogs, sliced
- ½ cup shredded sharp cheddar cheese
- 2 Tbsp. finely chopped pickled jalapeno, optional

1. Preheat oven to 400°. Line nine muffin cups with foil liners or grease nine non-stick muffin cups.
2. In a small bowl, combine muffin mix, milk and egg; stir in hot dogs, cheese and, if desired, jalapeno. Fill the prepared cups three-fourths full.
3. Bake 14-18 minutes or until a toothpick inserted in center comes out clean. Cool for 5 minutes before removing from pan to a wire rack. Serve warm. Refrigerate any leftovers.
Freeze option: Freeze cooled muffins in resealable plastic freezer bags. To use, microwave each muffin on high for 30-60 seconds or until heated through.
1 muffin: 216 cal., 10g fat (4g sat. fat), 46mg chol., 619mg sod., 23g carb. (7g sugars, 2g fiber), 8g pro.

SHREDDED GINGERED BRUSSELS SPROUTS

Even people who normally don't care for Brussels sprouts will ask for a second helping of these!
—James Schend, Pleasant Prairie, WI

Takes: 25 min. • **Makes:** 6 servings

- 1 lb. fresh Brussels sprouts (about 5½ cups)
- 1 Tbsp. olive oil
- 1 small onion, finely chopped
- 1 Tbsp. minced fresh gingerroot
- 1 garlic clove, minced
- ½ tsp. salt
- 2 Tbsp. water
- ¼ tsp. pepper

1. Trim Brussels sprouts. Cut sprouts lengthwise in half; cut crosswise into thin slices.
2. Place a large skillet over medium-high heat. Add Brussels sprouts; cook and stir for 2-3 minutes or until sprouts begin to brown lightly. Add oil and toss to coat. Stir in onion, ginger, garlic and salt. Add water; reduce heat to medium and cook, covered, 1-2 minutes or until vegetables are tender. Stir in pepper.
¾ cup: 56 cal., 2g fat (0 sat. fat), 0 chol., 214mg sod., 8g carb. (2g sugars, 3g fiber), 2g pro. **Diabetic exchanges:** 1 vegetable, ½ fat.

Sesame-Ginger Brussels Sprouts
Substitute toasted sesame oil for olive oil and proceed as directed. Sprinkle 1 Tbsp. toasted sesame seeds over the cooked sprouts before serving.

Cranberry-Pecan Brussels Sprouts
Add ¼ cup dried cranberries with the onion and ginger. Cook as directed; sprinkle sprouts with 2 Tbsp. chopped toasted pecans before serving.

Curry Brussels Sprouts Add 1 tsp. curry powder with the onion and ginger; cook Brussels sprouts as directed.

SHREDDED GINGERED BRUSSELS SPROUTS

CHEESE SMASHED POTATOES

CHEESE SMASHED POTATOES

Who doesn't like mashed potatoes? Try this slimmed-down dish with any entree.
—Janet Homes, Surprise, AZ

Prep: 10 min. • **Cook:** 25 min.
Makes: 4 servings

- 1 lb. small red potatoes, quartered
- 1 cup fresh cauliflowerets
- ⅔ cup shredded reduced-fat cheddar cheese
- ¼ cup reduced-fat sour cream
- ¼ tsp. salt

1. Place potatoes in a large saucepan and cover with water. Bring to a boil. Reduce heat; cover and cook 10 minutes. Add cauliflower; cook 10 minutes longer or until the vegetables are tender.
2. Drain; mash with cheese, sour cream and salt.

¾ cup: 161 cal., 5g fat (3g sat. fat), 18mg chol., 292mg sod., 21g carb. (3g sugars, 3g fiber), 8g pro. **Diabetic exchanges:** 1 starch, 1 medium-fat meat.

CHERRY TOMATO MOZZARELLA SAUTE

Cherry tomatoes and mozzarella are a perfect pairing. You're probably used to them raw, but cooking lightly with some aromatics really brings the flavor of tomatoes to its peak.
—Summer Jones, Pleasant Grove, UT

Takes: 25 min. • **Makes:** 4 servings

- 2 tsp. olive oil
- ¼ cup chopped shallots
- 1 tsp. minced fresh thyme
- 1 garlic clove, minced
- 2½ cups cherry tomatoes, halved
- ¼ tsp. salt
- ¼ tsp. pepper
- 4 oz. fresh mozzarella cheese cut into ½-in. cubes

In a large skillet, heat oil over medium-high heat; saute the shallots with thyme until tender. Add the garlic; cook and stir for 1 minute. Stir in tomatoes, salt and pepper; heat through. Remove from the heat; stir in cheese.

⅔ cup: 127 cal., 9g fat (4g sat. fat), 22mg chol., 194mg sod., 6g carb. (4g sugars, 2g fiber), 6g pro.

ROASTED SWEET POTATO WEDGES

ROASTED SWEET POTATO WEDGES

Sweet potatoes roasted with curry and smoked paprika delight everybody at our table. The mango chutney makes a sweet and tangy dip.

—Maitreyi Jois, Streamwood, IL

Takes: 25 min. • **Makes:** 4 servings

- 2 medium sweet potatoes (about 1 lb.), cut into ½-in. wedges
- 2 Tbsp. olive oil
- 1 tsp. curry powder
- ½ tsp. salt
- ½ tsp. smoked paprika
- ⅛ tsp. coarsely ground pepper
  Minced fresh cilantro
  Mango chutney, optional

1. Preheat oven to 425°. Place sweet potatoes in a large bowl. Mix oil and seasonings; drizzle over sweet potatoes and toss to coat. Transfer to an ungreased 15x10x1-in. baking pan.

2. Roast 15-20 minutes or until tender, turning occasionally. Sprinkle with cilantro. If desired, serve with chutney.
1 serving: 159 cal., 7g fat (1g sat. fat), 0 chol., 305mg sod., 23g carb. (9g sugars, 3g fiber), 2g pro. **Diabetic exchanges:** 1½ starch, 1½ fat.

MINTED BEET SALAD

We have neighbors who share vegetables from their garden, and every year my husband and I look forward to their beets. The sweetness of the beets is toned down by the vinegar and oil dressing with fresh mint. Kalamata olives add a salty touch.

—Barb Estabrook, Appleton, WI

Prep: 20 min.
Cook: 15 min. + chilling
Makes: 6 servings

- 5 medium fresh beets (about 2 lbs.)
- 2 Tbsp. water
- 2 Tbsp. champagne vinegar or rice vinegar
- 2 Tbsp. olive oil
- ½ tsp. salt
- ¼ tsp. coarsely ground pepper
- ¼ cup pitted kalamata olives, quartered
- 2 Tbsp. thinly sliced fresh mint, divided

1. Scrub beets; trim tops to 1 in. Place in a single layer in a large microwave-safe dish. Drizzle with water. Microwave, covered, on high for 14-15 minutes or until easily pierced with a fork, turning once; let stand 5 minutes.
2. When cool enough to handle, peel and cut beets into ¾-in. pieces. In a bowl, whisk vinegar, oil, salt and pepper until blended. Add olives, beets and 1 Tbsp. mint; toss to coat. Refrigerate, covered, at least 1 hour or until cold. Top with the remaining mint.
½ cup: 123 cal., 6g fat (1g sat. fat), 0 chol., 406mg sod., 16g carb. (12g sugars, 3g fiber), 3g pro. **Diabetic exchanges:** 1 vegetable, 1 fat.

PARMESAN-RANCH PAN ROLLS

My mom taught me this easy and delicious recipe, which is great for feeding a crowd—but they never leave anything for the next day. Mom used her homemade bread dough, but using frozen dough is my own busy-cook shortcut.
—Trisha Kruse, Eagle, ID

Prep: 30 min. + rising • **Bake:** 20 min.
Makes: 1½ dozen

- 2 loaves (1 lb. each) frozen bread dough, thawed
- 1 cup grated Parmesan cheese
- ½ cup butter, melted
- 1 envelope buttermilk ranch salad dressing mix
- 1 small onion, finely chopped

1. On a lightly floured surface, divide dough into 18 portions; shape each into a ball. In a small bowl, combine the cheese, butter and ranch dressing mix.
2. Roll balls in cheese mixture; arrange in two greased 9-in. square baking pans. Sprinkle with onion. Cover rolls and let rise in a warm place until doubled, about 45 minutes.
3. Meanwhile, preheat oven to 350°. Bake for 20-25 minutes or until golden brown. Remove from pans to wire racks.
1 serving: 210 cal., 8g fat (4g sat. fat), 17mg chol., 512mg sod., 26g carb. (2g sugars, 2g fiber), 7g pro.

BROCCOLI WITH GARLIC, BACON & PARMESAN

My approach to broccoli is to cook it slowly in a broth with garlic and smoky bacon so the flavors come together. Ordinary broccoli become irresistible.
—Erin Chilcoat, Central Islip, NY

Takes: 30 min. • **Makes:** 8 servings

- 1 tsp. salt
- 2 bunches broccoli (about 3 lbs.), stems removed, cut into florets
- 6 thick-sliced bacon strips, chopped
- 2 Tbsp. olive oil
- 6 to 8 garlic cloves, thinly sliced
- ½ tsp. crushed red pepper flakes
- ¼ cup shredded Parmesan cheese

1. Fill a 6-qt. stockpot two-thirds full with water; add salt and bring to a boil over high heat. In batches, add broccoli and cook for 2-3 minutes or until the broccoli turns bright green; remove with a slotted spoon.
2. In a large skillet, cook the bacon over medium heat until crisp, stirring occasionally. Remove with a slotted spoon; drain on paper towels. Discard drippings, reserving 1 Tbsp. in pan.
3. Add oil to drippings; heat over medium heat. Add garlic and pepper flakes; cook and stir for 2-3 minutes or until garlic is fragrant (do not allow to brown). Add broccoli; cook until the broccoli is tender, stirring occasionally. Stir in the bacon; sprinkle with cheese.
¾ cup: 155 cal., 10g fat (3g sat. fat), 11mg chol., 371mg sod., 11g carb. (3g sugars, 4g fiber), 8g pro. **Diabetic exchanges:** 2 fat, 1 vegetable.

✱
TEST KITCHEN TIP
The round, floppy rubber jar openers you find in stores have a great second use as a garlic peeler. Place a clove of garlic on the jar opener, wrap it around the garlic, then roll. It peels the garlic in a jiffy.

PARMESAN-RANCH PAN ROLLS

MARINATED ASPARAGUS WITH BLUE CHEESE

Asparagus marinated in vinaigrette and dotted with cheese makes an awesome side. We're blue cheese fans, but you might like Parmesan or feta instead.
—Susan Vaith, Jacksonville, FL

Prep: 20 min. + marinating
Makes: 4 servings

- 1 lb. fresh asparagus, trimmed
- 4 green onions, thinly sliced
- ¼ cup olive oil
- 2 Tbsp. white wine vinegar
- 1 garlic clove, minced
- ½ tsp. salt
- ¼ tsp. pepper
- ½ cup crumbled blue cheese

1. In a large saucepan, bring 6 cups water to a boil. Add asparagus; cook, uncovered, 2-3 minutes or just until crisp-tender. Remove asparagus and immediately drop into ice water. Drain and pat dry.
2. In a large resealable plastic bag, combine green onions, oil, vinegar, garlic, salt and pepper. Add the asparagus; seal bag and turn to coat. Refrigerate for at least 1 hour.
3. Drain asparagus, discarding marinade. Place asparagus spears on a serving plate; sprinkle with cheese.
1 serving: 136 cal., 12g fat (4g sat. fat), 13mg chol., 348mg sod., 3g carb. (1g sugars, 1g fiber), 5g pro.

TEST KITCHEN TIP
To trim asparagus, first rinse the stalks well in cold water. Then gently bend each one, letting it snap at a natural breaking point. Alternatively, you can use a knife to cut off the tough white bottom portion.

JASMINE RICE WITH COCONUT & CHERRIES

Our favorite rice deserves a bit of color and sweetness. We add cherries, peanuts, orange peel and coconut. That does the trick.
—Joy Zacharia, Clearwater, FL

Prep: 10 min. • **Cook:** 20 min. + standing
Makes: 4 servings

- 2½ cups water
- 1 Tbsp. olive oil
- ¾ tsp. salt
- 1½ cups uncooked jasmine rice
- ⅓ cup dried cherries
- ¼ cup chopped salted peanuts
- 1 tsp. grated orange zest
- ¼ cup sweetened shredded coconut, toasted

1. In a large saucepan, bring water, oil and salt to a boil. Stir in rice; return to a boil, stirring once. Reduce heat; simmer, covered, 15-17 minutes or until the water is absorbed.
2. Stir in cherries, peanuts and orange zest; let stand, covered, 10 minutes. Sprinkle with coconut.
Note: To toast coconut, bake in a shallow pan in a 350° oven for 5-10 minutes or cook in a skillet over low heat until golden brown, stirring occasionally.
1 cup: 411 cal., 10g fat (3g sat. fat), 0 chol., 498mg sod., 71g carb. (10g sugars, 3g fiber), 7g pro.

ORANGE POMEGRANATE SALAD WITH HONEY

ORANGE POMEGRANATE SALAD WITH HONEY

I discovered this pretty, fragrant salad in a cooking class. If you can, try to find some orange flower water (also called orange blossom water), which perks up the orange segments. But orange juice adds a nice zip, too!
—Carol Richardson Marty, Lynwood, WA

Takes: 15 min. • **Makes:** 6 servings

- 5 medium oranges or 10 clementines
- ½ cup pomegranate seeds
- 2 Tbsp. honey
- 1 to 2 tsp. orange flower water or orange juice

1. Cut a thin slice from the top and bottom of each orange; stand orange upright on a cutting board. With a knife, cut off peel and outer membrane from oranges. Cut crosswise into ½-in. slices.
2. Arrange orange slices on a serving platter; sprinkle with pomegranate seeds. In a small bowl, mix honey and orange flower water; drizzle over fruit.
⅔ cup: 62 cal., 0 fat (0 sat. fat), 0 chol., 2mg sod., 15g carb. (14g sugars, 0 fiber), 1g pro. **Diabetic exchanges:** 1 fruit.

MONKEY BREAD BISCUITS

Monkey bread is often a sweetly spiced breakfast treat. I came up with an easy dinner version featuring garlic and Italian seasoning the crowd will love.
—Dana Johnson, Scottsdale, AZ

Takes: 20 min. • **Makes:** 1 dozen

- 1 tube (16.3 oz.) large refrigerated flaky biscuits
- 3 Tbsp. butter, melted
- 1 garlic clove, minced
- ½ tsp. Italian seasoning
- ¼ cup grated Parmesan cheese Additional Italian seasoning

1. Preheat oven to 425°. Separate biscuits; cut each into six pieces. In a large bowl, combine butter, garlic and Italian seasoning; add biscuit pieces and toss to coat.
2. Place four pieces in each of 12 greased muffin cups. Sprinkle with cheese and additional Italian seasoning. Bake biscuits for 8-10 minutes or until golden brown. Serve warm.
1 biscuit: 159 cal., 9g fat (3g sat. fat), 9mg chol., 418mg sod., 16g carb. (3g sugars, 1g fiber), 3g pro.

CITRUS AVOCADO
SPINACH SALAD

GREEN OLIVE FOCACCIA

*Green olives complement my speedy
version of this beloved Italian bread.
Try it with minestrone or Italian wedding
soup, or serve it with an antipasto tray
for a hearty appetizer.*
—Ivy Laffoon, Ceres, CA

Takes: 30 min. • **Makes:** 8 servings

- 1 loaf (1 lb.) frozen bread dough, thawed
- ½ cup sliced pimiento-stuffed olives
- ½ cup shredded Colby-Monterey Jack cheese
- ½ cup shredded Parmesan cheese
- 1 tsp. Italian seasoning
- 2 Tbsp. olive oil

1. Preheat the oven to 350°. On an
ungreased baking sheet, pat dough into
a 12x6-in. rectangle. Build up the edges
slightly. Top with olives, cheeses and
Italian seasoning; press gently into dough.
Drizzle with oil.
2. Bake for 15-20 minutes or until cheese
is melted and golden brown. Let stand for
5 minutes before slicing.
1 slice: 249 cal., 11g fat (3g sat. fat),
10mg chol., 623mg sod., 31g carb. (2g
sugars, 2g fiber), 9g pro.

CITRUS AVOCADO SPINACH SALAD

*Tossing this salad together with creamy
avocado and tangy citrus is so simple, and
you don't even need to peel the oranges.*
—Karole Friemann, Kimberling City, MO

Prep: 15 min. • **Makes:** 8 servings

- 8 cups fresh baby spinach (about 6 oz.)
- 3 cups refrigerated citrus salad, drained
- 2 medium ripe avocados, peeled and sliced
- 1 cup crumbled blue cheese
  Sliced almonds, toasted, and salad dressing of your choice, optional

Divide spinach among eight plates; top
with citrus salad and avocados. Sprinkle
with cheese and, if desired, almonds and
dressing. Serve immediately.
Note: To toast nuts, bake in a shallow
pan in a 350° oven for 5-10 minutes or
cook in a skillet over low heat until lightly
browned, stirring occasionally. This recipe
was tested with Del Monte SunFresh
Citrus Salad.

1 serving: 168 cal., 10g fat (4g sat. fat),
13mg chol., 231mg sod., 16g carb. (10g
sugars, 3g fiber), 5g pro.

HAWAIIAN BARBECUE BEANS

*Fresh ginger is the secret ingredient in this
recipe. Guests rave when we serve it.*
—Helen Reynolds, Quincy, CA

Prep: 10 min. • **Cook:** 5 hours
Makes: 9 servings

- 4 cans (15 oz. each) black beans, rinsed and drained
- 1 can (20 oz.) crushed pineapple, drained
- 1 bottle (18 oz.) barbecue sauce
- 1½ tsp. minced fresh gingerroot
- ½ lb. bacon strips, cooked and crumbled

In a 4-qt. slow cooker, combine beans,
pineapple, barbecue sauce and ginger.
Cover and cook on low, 5-6 hours. Stir
in bacon before serving.
¾ cup: 286 cal., 5g fat (1g sat. fat), 9mg
chol., 981mg sod., 47g carb. (20g sugars,
9g fiber), 13g pro.

PEAR & BLUE CHEESE SALAD

*This crisp fall salad gets its tartness from
fresh pears, extra crunch from pecans
and a hint of creaminess from the blue
cheese. It's simple, but always impresses.*
—*Taste of Home* Test Kitchen

Takes: 10 min. • **Makes:** 10 servings

- 12 cups torn romaine
- ⅔ cup balsamic vinaigrette
- 2 medium pears, sliced
- ⅔ cup crumbled blue cheese
- ⅔ cup glazed pecans

Place romaine in a large bowl. Drizzle with
vinaigrette; toss to coat. Top with pears,
cheese and pecans. Serve immediately.
1 cup: 133 calories, 8g fat (2g saturated
fat), 7mg cholesterol, 324mg sodium, 12g
carbohydrate (8g sugars, 3g fiber), 3g
protein. **Diabetic Exchanges:** 1½ fat,
1 vegetable, ½ starch.

GREEN OLIVE FOCACCIA

BACON PEA SALAD

BACON PEA SALAD

My husband absolutely loves peas. My middle son isn't the biggest fan, but he loves bacon. So I combined the two, and it was perfect! This salad is an awesome side dish, especially for barbecue.
—Angela Lively, Conroe, TX

Prep: 10 min. + chilling
Makes: 6 servings

- 4 cups frozen peas (about 16 oz.), thawed
- ½ cup shredded sharp cheddar cheese
- ½ cup ranch salad dressing
- ⅓ cup chopped red onion
- ¼ tsp. salt
- ¼ tsp. pepper
- 4 bacon strips, cooked and crumbled

Combine the first six ingredients; toss to coat. Refrigerate, covered, at least 30 minutes. Stir in bacon before serving.
¾ cup: 218 cal., 14g fat (4g sat. fat), 17mg chol., 547mg sod., 14g carb. (6g sugars, 4g fiber), 9g pro.

BUTTERY SOUR CREAM MUFFINS

With just three ingredients you can round out a lovely meal with these butter-rich muffins. They taste like old-fashioned biscuits and practically melt in your mouth.
—Mary Cleckley, Slaton, TX

Takes: 30 min. • **Makes:** 3 servings

- ½ cup self-rising flour
- ¼ cup butter, melted
- ¼ cup sour cream
- 1 Tbsp. water

Preheat oven to 350°. In a small bowl, mix all ingredients just until moistened. Coat muffin cups with cooking spray; fill three-fourths full. Bake 18-20 minutes or until a toothpick inserted in center comes out clean. Cool for 5 minutes before removing from pan to a wire rack. Serve warm.
Note: As a substitute for self-rising flour, place ¾ tsp. baking powder and ¼ tsp. salt in a ½ cup measuring cup. Add all-purpose flour to measure ½ cup.
1 muffin: 272 cal., 22g fat (14g sat. fat), 61mg chol., 459mg sod., 16g carb. (1g sugars, 0 fiber), 4g pro.

PASSOVER POPOVERS

Popovers have an important role at the Passover table, substituting for bread. When puffed and golden brown, they're ready to share.
—Gloria Mezikofsky, Wakefield, MA

Prep: 25 min. • **Bake:** 20 min. + standing
Makes: 1 dozen

- 1 cup water
- ½ cup safflower oil
- ⅛ to ¼ tsp. salt
- 1 cup matzo cake meal
- 7 large eggs

1. Preheat oven to 450°. Generously grease 12 muffin cups. In a large saucepan, bring water, oil and salt to a rolling boil. Add cake meal all at once and beat until blended. Remove from heat; let stand 5 minutes.

2. Transfer mixture to a blender. Add two eggs; process, covered, until blended. Continue adding eggs, one at a time, and process until incorporated. Process 2 minutes longer or until mixture is smooth.

3. Fill the prepared muffin cups three-fourths full. Bake 18-22 minutes or until puffed, very firm and golden brown. Turn off oven (do not open oven door); leave popovers in the oven 10 minutes. Then, remove pan from oven and immediately remove popovers from pan to a wire rack. Serve hot.

Note: This recipe was tested with Manischewitz cake meal. Look for it in the baking aisle or kosher foods section.

1 popover: 174 cal., 12g fat (2g sat. fat), 109mg chol., 66mg sod., 11g carb. (0 sugars, 0 fiber), 5g pro.

PASSOVER
POPOVERS

GINGERBREAD & PUMPKIN CREAM TRIFLE
PG 103

Sweets & Desserts

Cookies, cupcakes, pies and other after-dinner delights make for impressive edibles any night of the week. Get ready to be amazed!

CHOCOLATE-DIPPED STRAWBERRY MERINGUE ROSES

CHOCOLATE-DIPPED STRAWBERRY MERINGUE ROSES

Eat these pretty treats as is, or crush them into a bowl of strawberries and whipped cream. Readers of my blog, utry.it, *went nuts when I posted that idea.*
—Amy Tong, Anaheim, CA

Prep: 25 min. • **Bake:** 40 min. + cooling
Makes: 2 dozen

- 3   large egg whites
- ¼   cup sugar
- ¼   cup freeze-dried strawberries
- 1   pkg. (3 oz.) strawberry gelatin
- ½   tsp. vanilla extract, optional
- 1   cup 60% cacao bittersweet chocolate baking chips, melted

1. Place egg whites in a large bowl; let stand at room temperature 30 minutes. Preheat oven to 225°.
2. Place sugar and strawberries in a food processor; process until powdery. Add gelatin; pulse to blend.
3. Beat egg whites on medium speed until foamy, adding vanilla if desired. Gradually add the gelatin mixture, 1 Tbsp. at a time, beating on high after each addition until the sugar is dissolved. Continue beating until stiff glossy peaks form.
4. Cut a small hole in the tip of a pastry bag or in a corner of a food-safe plastic bag; insert a #1M star tip. Transfer the meringue to the bag. Pipe 2-in. roses 1½ in. apart onto parchment paper-lined baking sheets.
5. Bake for 40-45 minutes or until set and dry. Turn off oven (do not open the oven door); leave meringues in oven for 1½ hours. Remove from oven; cool completely on baking sheets.
6. Remove meringues from paper. Dip bottoms in melted chocolate; allow excess chocolate to drip off. Place on waxed paper; let stand until set, about 45 minutes. Store in an airtight container at room temperature.

1 cookie: 33 cal., 1g fat (1g sat. fat), 0 chol., 9mg sod., 6g carb. (5g sugars, 0 fiber), 1g pro. **Diabetic exchanges:** ½ starch.

TEST KITCHEN TIP
Humidity is the most critical factor when making a successful meringue, so choose a dry day. On a humid day, meringues can absorb moisture and become limp and sticky.

SHOOFLY CUPCAKES

These moist old-fashioned molasses cupcakes were my grandmother's specialty. To keep them from all disappearing too quickly, she used to store them out of sight. Somehow, we always figured out her hiding places!
—Beth Adams, Jacksonville, FL

Prep: 15 min. • **Bake:** 20 min. + cooling
Makes: 2 dozen

- 4 **cups all-purpose flour**
- 2 **cups packed brown sugar**
- ¼ **tsp. salt**
- 1 **cup cold butter, cubed**
- 2 **tsp. baking soda**
- 2 **cups boiling water**
- 1 **cup molasses**

1. Preheat oven to 350°. In a large bowl, combine flour, brown sugar and salt. Cut in butter until crumbly. Set aside 1 cup for topping. Add baking soda to the remaining crumb mixture. Stir in water and molasses.

2. Fill paper-lined muffin cups two-thirds full. Sprinkle with the reserved crumb mixture. Bake 20-25 minutes or until a toothpick inserted in the center comes out clean. Cool for 10 minutes before removing from pans to wire racks to cool completely.

Note: This recipe does not use eggs.

1 serving: 248 cal., 8g fat (5g sat. fat), 20mg chol., 219mg sod., 43g carb. (26g sugars, 1g fiber), 2g pro.

SHOOFLY
CUPCAKES

Family Classic

ICE CREAM
KOLACHKES

ICE CREAM KOLACHKES

These sweet pastries (also spelled kolaches) have Polish and Czech roots and are usually filled with poppy seeds, nuts, jam or a mashed fruit mixture. The ice cream is a twist on traditional kolachkes. It's simplest to use a square cookie cutter to cut the dough.
—Diane Turner, Brunswick, OH

Prep: 1 hour + chilling
Bake: 15 min./batch
Makes: 10 dozen

- 2 cups butter, softened
- 1 pint vanilla ice cream, softened
- 4 cups all-purpose flour
- 2 Tbsp. sugar
- 2 cans (12 oz. each) apricot and/or raspberry cake and pastry filling
- 1 to 2 Tbsp. confectioners' sugar, optional

1. In the bowl of a heavy-duty stand mixer, beat butter and ice cream until blended (mixture will appear curdled). Add flour and sugar; mix well. Divide dough into four portions; cover and refrigerate for 2 hours or until easy to handle.
2. Preheat oven to 350°. On a lightly floured surface, roll one portion of dough into a 12x10–in. rectangle; cut into 2-in. squares. Place a teaspoonful of filling in the center of each square. Overlap two opposite corners of dough over filling; pinch tightly to seal. Place 2 in. apart on ungreased baking sheets. Repeat with the remaining dough and filling.
3. Bake 11-14 minutes or until bottoms are lightly browned. Cool for 1 minute before removing from pans to wire racks. Sprinkle the pastries with confectioners' sugar if desired.
Note: This recipe was tested with Solo brand cake and pastry filling. Look for it in the baking aisle.
1 kolachke: 60 cal., 3g fat (2g sat. fat), 9mg chol., 27mg sod., 7g carb. (2g sugars, 0 fiber), 1g pro. **Diabetic exchanges:** ½ starch, ½ fat.

NO-BAKE CEREAL BARS

NO-BAKE CEREAL BARS

Made with peanut butter and two kinds of cereal, these bars taste almost like candy!
—Pauline Christiansen, Columbus, KS

Takes: 20 min. • **Makes:** about 10 dozen

- 2 cups sugar
- 2 cups corn syrup
- 1 jar (40 oz.) chunky peanut butter
- 6 cups Cheerios
- 6 cups Rice Chex

Lightly grease two 15x10x1-in. pans; set aside. In a large saucepan, cook and stir sugar and corn syrup until the sugar is dissolved. Remove from the heat. Add peanut butter; mix well. Stir in cereals. Quickly spread into the prepared pans. Cut into bars while warm.
1 bar: 95 cal., 5g fat (1g sat. fat), 0 chol., 79mg sod., 12g carb. (7g sugars, 1g fiber), 3g pro.

PEANUT BUTTER FUDGE

This is a favorite "never-fail" recipe, and with only three ingredients, it couldn't be quicker or simpler to make.
—Eleanore Peterson, Fort Atkinson, WI

Prep: 10 min. + chilling • **Makes:** 1¾ lbs.

- 1 lb. white candy coating
- 1 cup creamy peanut butter
- 1 cup coarsely chopped walnuts

Grease an 8-in. square pan; set aside. Melt coating in a saucepan over medium-low heat, stirring constantly until smooth. Remove from the heat; stir in peanut butter and walnuts. Spread into the prepared pan. Chill until firm, then cut into 1-in. squares.
2 pieces: 147 cal., 10g fat (5g sat. fat), 0 chol., 37mg sod., 12g carb. (10g sugars, 1g fiber), 3g pro.

EASY FRESH
STRAWBERRY
PIE

EASY FRESH STRAWBERRY PIE

For my mother's 70th birthday and Mother's Day, I made two of these pies instead of a cake. Since it was mid-May in Texas, the berries were absolutely perfect. It was a memorable occasion for the whole family.
—Josh Carter, Birmingham, AL

Prep: 20 min. + cooling
Bake: 15 min. + chilling
Makes: 8 servings

 1   unbaked pie crust (9 in.)
 ¾   cup sugar
 2   Tbsp. cornstarch
 1   cup water
 1   pkg. (3 oz.) strawberry gelatin
 4   cups sliced fresh strawberries
     Fresh mint, optional
     Whipped cream, optional

1. Line unpricked pie crust with a double thickness of heavy-duty foil. Bake at 450° for 8 minutes. Remove the foil; bake 5 minutes longer. Cool crust on a wire rack.
2. In a small saucepan, combine sugar, cornstarch and water until smooth. Bring to a boil; cook and stir for 2 minutes or until thickened. Remove from the heat; stir in gelatin until dissolved. Refrigerate for 15-20 minutes or until slightly cooled.
3. Meanwhile, arrange strawberries in the crust. Pour the gelatin mixture over the berries. Refrigerate until set. Garnish with mint if desired.
1 slice: 264 cal., 7g fat (3g sat. fat), 5mg chol., 125mg sod., 49g carb. (32g sugars, 2g fiber), 2g pro.

TEST KITCHEN TIP

For another presentation, use fresh whole strawberries and arrange them point-side up in the crust. It not only looks beautiful but also saves time slicing the berries.

GINGERBREAD & PUMPKIN CREAM TRIFLE

We wait for these flavors all year long. Stack up the layers in a big trifle bowl, or make minis for everybody at the table.
—Amy Geiser, Fairlawn, OH

Prep: 45 min. + chilling
Makes: 10 servings

- 1 pkg. (14½ oz.) gingerbread cake/cookie mix
- 1 pkg. (3 oz.) cook-and-serve vanilla pudding mix
- ¼ cup packed brown sugar
- 1⅔ cups canned pumpkin pie mix
- 1 carton (8 oz.) frozen whipped topping, thawed
  Optional toppings: caramel topping, toasted pecans and gingersnap cookies

1. Prepare and bake gingerbread cake according to package directions. Cool completely on a wire rack.

2. Meanwhile, prepare the pudding mix according to package directions; stir in brown sugar and pie mix. Transfer to a bowl; refrigerate, covered, 30 minutes.

3. Cut or break gingerbread into ¾-in. pieces. In ten 12-oz. glasses or a 3-qt. trifle bowl, layer half of each of the following: cake, pumpkin mixture and whipped topping. Repeat the layers. Refrigerate, covered, for 4 hours or overnight. Top as desired.

1 serving: 372 cal., 11g fat (6g sat. fat), 23mg chol., 414mg sod., 61g carb. (44g sugars, 2g fiber), 5g pro.

YUMMY CRACKER SNACKS

These treats are my family's favorite, and it seems no matter how many I make, they always disappear too soon. It's a good thing it's so easy to make more!
—D. Weaver, Ephrata, PA

Prep: 1 hour + chilling
Makes: 4 dozen

- 96 Ritz crackers
- 1 cup creamy peanut butter
- 1 cup marshmallow creme
- 2 lbs. milk chocolate candy coating, melted
  Holiday sprinkles, optional

1. Spread half the crackers with peanut butter. Spread remaining crackers with marshmallow creme; place creme side down over peanut butter crackers.

2. Dip in melted candy coating; allow excess to drip off. Place on waxed paper-lined pans; refrigerate for 15 minutes or until set. Drizzle with additional candy coating and decorate with sprinkles. Store cracker snacks in an airtight container.

1 cracker snack: 170 cal., 10g fat (6g sat. fat), 0 chol., 89mg sod., 19g carb. (14g sugars, 1g fiber), 2g pro.

BAKED CUSTARD WITH CINNAMON

Mother used to make this comforting custard when I was growing up on the farm. It was wonderful after a chilly evening of doing chores. Now I fix it for my husband and four sons.
—Mary Kay Morris, Cokato, MN

Prep: 10 min.
Bake: 50 min. + cooling
Makes: 4 servings

- 2 large eggs
- 2 cups whole milk
- ⅓ cup sugar
- ¼ tsp. salt
  Dash ground cinnamon
  Dash ground nutmeg

1. In a small bowl, whisk the eggs, milk, sugar and salt. Pour into four ungreased 8-oz. custard cups; sprinkle with the cinnamon and nutmeg.

2. Place cups in a 13x9-in. baking pan; pour hot water into pan to a depth of ¾ in. Bake, uncovered, at 350° for 50-55 minutes or until a knife inserted in the center comes out clean. Remove cups to a wire rack to cool. Serve warm or chilled. Store in the refrigerator.

1 serving: 177 cal., 7g fat (3g sat. fat), 123mg chol., 239mg sod., 23g carb. (22g sugars, 0 fiber), 7g pro.

GINGERBREAD & PUMPKIN CREAM TRIFLE

AUNT ROSE'S FANTASTIC BUTTER TOFFEE

While I don't live in the country, I do love everything about it—especially good old-fashioned home cooking. Every year, you'll find me at our county fair, entering a different recipe contest. This toffee is a family favorite!
—Kathy Dorman, Snover, MI

Prep: 25 min.
Cook: 15 min.
Makes: about 2 lbs

- 2 cups unblanched whole almonds
- 11 oz. milk chocolate, chopped
- 1 cup butter, cubed
- 1 cup sugar
- 3 Tbsp. cold water

1. Preheat oven to 350°. In a shallow baking pan, toast almonds until golden brown, 5-10 minutes, stirring the nuts occasionally. Cool. Pulse chocolate in a food processor until finely ground (do not overprocess); transfer to a bowl. Pulse almonds in food processor until coarsely chopped. Sprinkle 1 cup of the almonds over the bottom of a greased 15x10x1-in. pan. Sprinkle with 1 cup of the chocolate.
2. In a heavy saucepan, combine butter, sugar and water. Cook over medium heat until a candy thermometer reads 290° (soft-crack stage), stirring occasionally.
3. Immediately pour mixture over the almonds and chocolate in the pan. Sprinkle with the remaining chocolate and almonds. Refrigerate until set; break into pieces.
Note: We recommend that you test your candy thermometer before each use by bringing water to a boil; the thermometer should read 212°. Adjust your recipe temperature based on the test.
1 oz.: 177 cal., 13g fat (6g sat. fat), 17mg chol., 51mg sod., 14g carb. (12g sugars, 1g fiber), 3g pro.

QUICK ICEBOX SANDWICHES

My mother liked making these cool, creamy treats when I was growing up in the States because they're so quick to fix. Then I made them for my own kids.
—Sandy Armijo, Naples, Italy

Prep: 20 min. + freezing • **Makes:** 2 dozen

- 1 pkg. (3.4 oz.) instant vanilla pudding mix
- 2 cups cold milk
- 2 cups whipped topping
- 1 cup miniature semisweet chocolate chips
- 24 whole graham crackers, halved

1. Mix pudding and milk according to the package directions; refrigerate until set. Fold in the whipped topping and chocolate chips.
2. Place 24 graham cracker halves on a baking sheet; top each with about 3 Tbsp. filling. Place another graham cracker half on top. Wrap each sandwich individually in plastic; freeze for 1 hour or until firm. Serve frozen.
1 sandwich: 144 cal., 5g fat (3g sat. fat), 3mg chol., 162mg sod., 23g carb. (13g sugars, 1g fiber), 2g pro.

TART CHERRY PIE

My aunt and I are diabetic, and we both enjoy this yummy fruit pie. Our friends even request it for dessert when they come to visit us.
—Bonnie Johnson, DeKalb, IL

Prep: 15 min. + cooling • **Makes:** 8 servings

- 2 cans (14½ oz. each) pitted tart cherries
- 1 pkg. (3 oz.) cook-and-serve vanilla pudding mix
- 1 pkg. (.3 oz.) sugar-free cherry gelatin
  Sugar substitute equivalent to 4 tsp. sugar
- 1 pie crust (9 in.), baked

Drain cherries, reserving the juice; set cherries aside. In a large saucepan, combine cherry juice and dry pudding mix. Cook and stir until mixture comes to a boil and is thickened and bubbly. Remove from heat; stir in gelatin powder and sweetener until dissolved. Stir in cherries; transfer to pie crust. Cool completely. Store in the refrigerator.
1 piece: 174 cal., 7g fat (3g sat. fat), 5mg chol., 162mg sod., 25g carb. (11g sugars, 1g fiber), 2g pro. **Diabetic exchanges:** 1 starch, 1 fat, ½ fruit.

QUICK ICEBOX SANDWICHES

APPLE KUCHEN BARS

APPLE KUCHEN BARS

This recipe is about family, comfort and simplicity. My mom made the bars, and now I bake them in my own kitchen—double batches so I can pass along the love!
—Elizabeth Monfort, Celina, OH

Prep: 35 min. • **Bake:** 1 hour + cooling
Makes: 2 dozen

  3 cups all-purpose flour, divided
  ¼ tsp. salt
  1½ cups cold butter, divided
  4 to 5 Tbsp. ice water
  8 cups thinly sliced peeled tart apples (about 8 medium)
  2 cups sugar, divided
  2 tsp. ground cinnamon

1. Preheat oven to 350°. Place 2 cups of flour and the salt in a food processor; pulse until blended. Add 1 cup butter; pulse until the butter is the size of peas. While pulsing, add just enough ice water to form moist crumbs. Press the mixture into bottom of a greased 13x9-in. baking pan. Bake 20-25 minutes or until edges are lightly browned. Cool on a wire rack.
2. In a large bowl, combine apples, 1 cup sugar and the cinnamon; toss to coat. Spoon apples over the crust. Place the remaining flour, butter and sugar in food processor; pulse until coarse crumbs form. Sprinkle over the apples. Bake for 60-70 minutes or until golden brown and the apples are tender. Cool completely on a wire rack. Cut into bars.
1 bar: 240 cal., 12g fat (7g sat. fat), 30mg chol., 106mg sod., 33g carb. (21g sugars, 1g fiber), 2g pro.

PULL-APART CARAMEL COFFEE CAKE

PULL-APART CARAMEL COFFEE CAKE

I made this delightful breakfast treat for a brunch party, and now I get requests every time family or friends do anything around the breakfast hour. I always keep the four simple ingredients on hand.
—Jaime Keeling, Keizer, OR

Prep: 10 min. • **Bake:** 25 min.
Makes: 1 loaf (16 servings)

- 2 tubes (12 oz. each) refrigerated buttermilk biscuits
- 1 cup packed brown sugar
- ½ cup heavy whipping cream
- 1 tsp. ground cinnamon

1. Preheat oven to 350°. Cut each biscuit into four pieces; arrange evenly in a 10-in. fluted tube pan coated with cooking spray. In a small bowl, mix the remaining ingredients until blended; pour over the biscuits.
2. Bake for 25-30 minutes or until golden brown. Cool in pan 5 minutes before inverting onto a serving plate.
5 pieces: 204 cal., 8g fat (3g sat. fat), 10mg chol., 457mg sod., 31g carb. (16g sugars, 0 fiber), 3g pro.

GERMAN PLUM TART

The buttery crust of this fruit-filled treat will simply melt in your mouth. You can substitute sliced apples or peaches for the plums with great results. I've also used fresh blueberries, It's wonderful to have a treat that's so simple and still tastes like something Grandma made.
—Helga Schlape, Florham Park, NJ

Prep: 10 min.
Bake: 35 min.
Makes: 8 servings

- ½ cup butter, softened
- 4 Tbsp. sugar, divided
- 1 large egg yolk
- ¾ to 1 cup all-purpose flour
- 2 lbs. plums, quartered (about 4 cups)

1. Preheat oven to 350°. In a small bowl, cream butter and 3 Tbsp. sugar until light and fluffy. Beat in egg yolk. Gradually add the flour, ¼ cup at a time, until the mixture forms a soft dough. Press dough into the bottom and up the sides of a 9-in. pie plate.
2. Arrange plums, skin side up with edges overlapping, in crust; sprinkle with the remaining sugar. Bake for 35-45 minutes or until the crust is golden brown and the fruit is tender.
1 serving: 237 cal., 13g fat (7g sat. fat), 57mg chol., 117mg sod., 30g carb. (18g sugars, 2g fiber), 3g pro.

LEMON CRISP COOKIES

Here's a quick-to-fix delight that's perfect to make when you've forgotten a treat for a bake sale or potluck. It only takes 10 minutes to whip up. The sunny yellow color, big lemon flavor and delightful crunch are sure to bring smiles.
—Julia Livingston, Frostproof, FL

Takes: 30 min. • **Makes:** about 4 dozen

- 1 pkg. lemon cake mix (regular size)
- 1 cup crisp rice cereal
- ½ cup butter, melted
- 1 large egg, lightly beaten
- 1 tsp. grated lemon peel

1. Preheat oven to 350°. In a large bowl, combine all the ingredients (dough will be crumbly). Shape into 1-in. balls. Place 2 in. apart on ungreased baking sheets.
2. Bake 10-12 minutes or until set. Cool 1 minute; remove from pan to a wire rack to cool completely.
2 cookies: 128 cal., 6g fat (3g sat. fat), 19mg chol., 189mg sod., 18g carb. (10g sugars, 0 fiber), 1g pro.

PEACH CRISP

I love crisps, and this one is a cinch to make. Rice Chex makes it unusual, while peaches and brown sugar provide loads of classic appeal. Better still, it takes less than 30 minutes from start to finish!
—Tracy Golder, Bloomsburg, PA

Takes: 25 min. • **Makes:** 6 servings

- 2 cans (15 oz. each) sliced peaches, drained
- 2 cups Rice Chex, crushed
- ⅓ cup packed brown sugar
- ¼ cup all-purpose flour
- 3 Tbsp. cold butter
  Whipped topping or ice cream, optional

1. Preheat oven to 375°. Place peaches in a greased 8-in. square baking dish. In a small bowl, combine the cereal, brown sugar and flour; cut in butter until mixture resembles coarse crumbs. Sprinkle over the peaches.
2. Bake for 15-20 minutes or until topping is golden brown. Serve warm.

1 serving: 222 cal., 6g fat (4g sat. fat), 15mg chol., 125mg sod., 41g carb. (30g sugars, 1g fiber), 1g pro.

EASY PISTACHIO BUNDT CAKE

Mixes make this light cake easy, and a fluted tube pan gets it party-ready. Go for the pistachios on top—the extra crunch is worth it.
—Dina Crowell, Fredericksburg, VA

Prep: 15 min. • **Bake:** 35 min. + cooling
Makes: 12 servings

- 1 pkg. yellow cake mix (regular size)
- 1 pkg. (3.4 oz.) instant pistachio pudding mix
- 4 large eggs
- 1½ cups water
- ¼ cup canola oil
- ½ tsp. almond extract
  Confectioners' sugar
  Finely chopped pistachios, optional

1. Preheat oven to 350°. Grease and flour a 10-in. fluted tube pan; set aside.
2. In a large bowl, combine the first six ingredients; beat on low speed for 30 seconds. Increase speed to medium and beat for 2 minutes. Transfer batter to prepared pan. Bake 35-40 minutes or until a toothpick inserted in center comes out clean. Cool in pan for 10 minutes before removing cake to a wire rack to cool completely.
3. Dust cake with confectioners' sugar. If desired, sprinkle with pistachios.
Note: To remove cakes easily, use solid shortening to grease plain and fluted tube pans.
1 slice: 266 cal., 10g fat (2g sat. fat), 62mg chol., 416mg sod., 41g carb. (24g sugars, 0 fiber), 4g pro.

✱
TEST KITCHEN TIP
If you like, you can make a frosting for this cake with 1 box pistachio pudding mix, 1¼ cups of 1% milk and 1 package Dream Whip. Whip for a few minutes with an electric mixer until soft peaks form.

LEMON CRISP COOKIES

STRAWBERRY SHORTCAKE STACKS

TURTLE PRALINE TART

This rich dessert is my own creation, and I'm very proud of it. It's easy enough to make for every day but special enough to serve guests or take to a potluck.
—Kathy Specht, Clinton, MT

Prep: 35 min. + chilling
Makes: 16 servings

- 1 sheet refrigerated pie crust
- 36 caramels
- 1 cup heavy whipping cream, divided
- 3½ cups pecan halves
- ½ cup semisweet chocolate chips, melted

1. Preheat oven to 450°. Unroll pie crust on a lightly floured surface. Transfer to an 11-in. fluted tart pan with removable bottom; trim edges.
2. Line unpricked pie crust with a double thickness of heavy-duty foil. Bake for 8 minutes. Remove foil; bake 5-6 minutes longer or until light golden brown. Cool on a wire rack.
3. In a large saucepan, combine caramels and ½ cup cream. Cook and stir over medium-low heat until the caramels are melted. Stir in pecans. Spread the filling evenly into the crust. Drizzle with melted chocolate.
4. Refrigerate 30 minutes or until set. Whip remaining cream; serve with tart.
1 slice: 335 cal., 24g fat (4g sat. fat), 4mg chol., 106mg sod., 31g carb. (19g sugars, 3g fiber), 4g pro.

★ ★ ★ ★ ★ **READER REVIEW**
"My husband drooled over the picture and thought the finished product was amazing!"
SCAMPHUYSEN TASTEOFHOME.COM

STRAWBERRY SHORTCAKE STACKS

When a friend brought me a pint of strawberries, I decided to make a shortcake with a pretty, elegant spin. These light and airy puff pastry stacks really let the fruit shine.
—Jenny Dubinsky, Inwood, WV

Prep: 25 min. • **Bake:** 15 min. + cooling
Makes: 12 servings

- 1 sheet frozen puff pastry, thawed
- 4 cups fresh strawberries, sliced
- ¼ cup plus 3 Tbsp. sugar, divided
- 1½ cups heavy whipping cream
- ½ tsp. vanilla extract

1. Preheat oven to 400°. On a lightly floured surface, roll puff pastry to a 10-in. square; cut into 12 rectangles (approx. 3x2½-in.). Place on ungreased baking sheets. Bake until golden brown, 12-15 minutes. Remove to wire racks to cool.
2. In a large bowl, toss strawberries with ¼ cup sugar. Let stand for 30 minutes, stirring occasionally. In another bowl, beat cream until it begins to thicken. Add vanilla and the remaining sugar; beat until stiff peaks form.
3. To serve, split pastries horizontally in half. Top each bottom half with 2 Tbsp. whipped cream and 1 Tbsp. strawberries; replace the top half. Top with the remaining whipped cream and strawberries.
1 serving: 246 calories, 16g fat (8g saturated fat), 34mg cholesterol, 76mg sodium, 23g carbohydrate (11g sugars, 2g fiber), 3g protein.

RECIPE INDEX

63

67

SUBSTITUTIONS & EQUIVALENTS

EQUIVALENT MEASURES

3 teaspoons	= 1 tablespoon	**16 tablespoons**	= 1 cup
4 tablespoons	= ¼ cup	**2 cups**	= 1 pint
5⅓ tablespoons	= ⅓ cup	**4 cups**	= 1 quart
8 tablespoons	= ½ cup	**4 quarts**	= 1 gallon

FOOD EQUIVALENTS

Macaroni	1 cup (3½ ounces) uncooked	= 2½ cups cooked
Noodles, Medium	3 cups (4 ounces) uncooked	= 4 cups cooked
Popcorn	⅓ - ½ cup unpopped	= 8 cups popped
Rice, Long Grain	1 cup uncooked	= 3 cups cooked
Rice, Quick-Cooking	1 cup uncooked	= 2 cups cooked
Spaghetti	8 ounces uncooked	= 4 cups cooked
Bread	1 slice	= ¾ cup soft crumbs, ¼ cup fine dry crumbs
Graham Crackers	7 squares	= ½ cup finely crushed
Buttery Round Crackers	12 crackers	= ½ cup finely crushed
Saltine Crackers	14 crackers	= ½ cup finely crushed
Bananas	1 medium	= ⅓ cup mashed
Lemons	1 medium	= 3 tablespoons juice, 2 teaspoons grated zest
Limes	1 medium	= 2 tablespoons juice, 1½ teaspoons grated zest
Oranges	1 medium	= ¼ -⅓ cup juice, 4 teaspoons grated zest

Cabbage	1 head = 5 cups shredded	**Green Pepper**	1 large = 1 cup chopped
Carrots	1 pound = 3 cups shredded	**Mushrooms**	½ pound = 3 cups sliced
Celery	1 rib = ½ cup chopped	**Onions**	1 medium = ½ cup chopped
Corn	1 ear fresh = ⅔ cup kernels	**Potatoes**	3 medium = 2 cups cubed
Almonds	1 pound = 3 cups chopped	**Pecan Halves**	1 pound = 4½ cups chopped
Ground Nuts	3¾ ounces = 1 cup	**Walnuts**	1 pound = 3¾ cups chopped

EASY SUBSTITUTIONS

CALLS FOR	AMOUNT	SUBSTITUTE
Baking Powder	1 teaspoon	½ teaspoon cream of tartar + ¼ teaspoon baking soda
Buttermilk	1 cup	1 tablespoon lemon juice or vinegar + enough milk to measure 1 cup (let stand 5 minutes before using)
Cornstarch	1 tablespoon	2 tablespoons all-purpose flour
Honey	1 cup	1¼ cups sugar + ¼ cup water
Half-and-Half Cream	1 cup	1 tablespoon melted butter + enough whole milk to measure 1 cup
Onion	1 small, chopped (⅓ cup)	1 teaspoon onion powder or 1 tablespoon dried minced onion
Tomato Juice	1 cup	½ cup tomato sauce + ½ cup water
Tomato Sauce	2 cups	¾ cup tomato paste + 1 cup water
Unsweetened Chocolate	1 square (1 ounce)	3 tablespoons baking cocoa + 1 tablespoon shortening or oil
Whole Milk	1 cup	½ cup evaporated milk + ½ cup water